Collins

Student Support Materials for AQA

AS/A-level Year 1

Biology

Topics 1 and 2: Biological molecules, Cells

Author: Mike Boyle

William Collins' dream of knowledge for all began with the publication of his first book in 1819.

A self-educated mill worker, he not only enriched millions of lives, but also founded a flourishing publishing house. Today, staying true to this spirit, Collins books are packed with inspiration, innovation and practical expertise. They place you at the centre of a world of possibility and give you exactly what you need to explore it.

Collins. Freedom to teach

HarperCollins Publishers
The News Building
1 London Bridge Street
London SE1 9GF

Browse the complete Collins catalogue at www.collins.co.uk

10 9 8 7 6 5 4 3 2 1

ISBN 978-0-00-818079-9

www.collins.co.uk

A catalogue record for this book is available from the British Library

Commissioned by Gillian Lindsey
Edited by Alexander Rutherford
Project managed by Maheswari PonSaravanan at Jouve
Development by Kate Redmond and Gillian Lindsey
Copyedited by Rebecca Ramsden
Proof read by Janette Schubert
Original design by Newgen Imaging
Typeset by Jouve India Private Limited
Cover design by Angela English
Printed by CPI Group (UK) Ltd, Croydon, CR0 4YY
Cover image © iStock/royaltystockphoto

Contents

3.1 Biological molecules

3.1.1 Monomers and polymers

Polymers are long, chain-like molecules made from simpler units called **monomers**. The carbohydrates starch, glycogen and cellulose are all polymers in which the monomer is glucose. As we shall see in 3.1.2, glucose is a 'simple sugar' or **monosaccharide**.

Protein molecules are also polymers made from a large number of **amino acid** monomers. **Nucleotides** including DNA and RNA also form polymers, joining together into long chains to form **polynucleotides**.

A **condensation** reaction is a reaction in which two molecules join, forming water in the process. Carbohydrates, lipids and proteins are all made by condensation reactions.

Breaking down polymers, such as in digestion of starch, usually involves a **hydrolysis** reaction. A hydrolysis reaction breaks down a compound by reacting with water.

3.1.2 Carbohydrates

Carbohydrates include **sugars**, **starches**, **cellulose** and **glycogen**. Carbohydrates always contain the elements carbon, hydrogen and oxygen, and can be divided into three categories according to size:

- **Monosaccharides** – 'single sugars', for example, glucose, fructose, galactose.
- **Disaccharides** – 'double sugars', for example, sucrose, maltose, lactose.
- **Polysaccharides** – 'multiple sugars', for example, starch, glycogen and cellulose.

Both mono- and disaccharides are classed as sugars and are sweet, white, water-soluble solids. Polysaccharides are polymers of sugars and are neither sweet nor soluble.

> **Definition**
>
> ***Polymers** are long, chain-like molecules made from simpler units called **monomers**. The carbohydrates starch, glycogen and cellulose are all polymers in which the monomer is glucose. Proteins are also polymers but lipids are not.*

Monosaccharides

The commonest monosaccharide is glucose, which exists in two forms: **α glucose** and **β glucose** (Fig 1). The different forms affect the properties of the polymers that contain glucose (see **Glycogen and cellulose** sub-section, page 7).

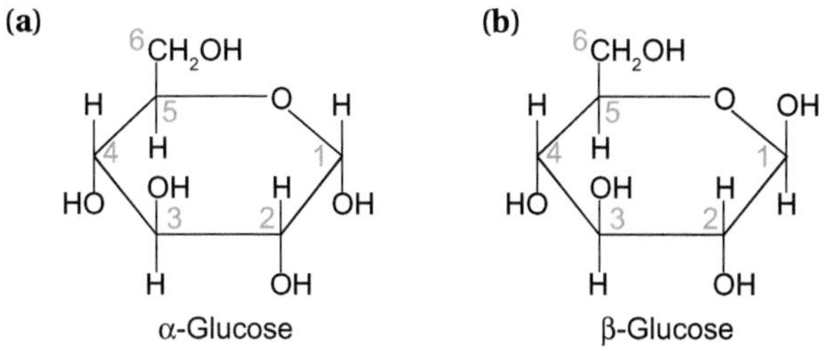

(a) α-Glucose (b) β-Glucose

Fig 1
The structure of α-glucose and β-glucose. The key difference is the position of the -OH group on carbons 1 and 4. This difference may look tiny, but α-glucose polymerises to form starch and glycogen, whereas β-glucose polymerises to form cellulose – molecules with completely different properties and functions.

Fig 2 shows how two glucose molecules join. They link by a **condensation reaction** that produces the disaccharide maltose along with one molecule of water. The two monosaccharides are linked by a **glycosidic bond** (C—O—C), where the molecules share an oxygen atom.

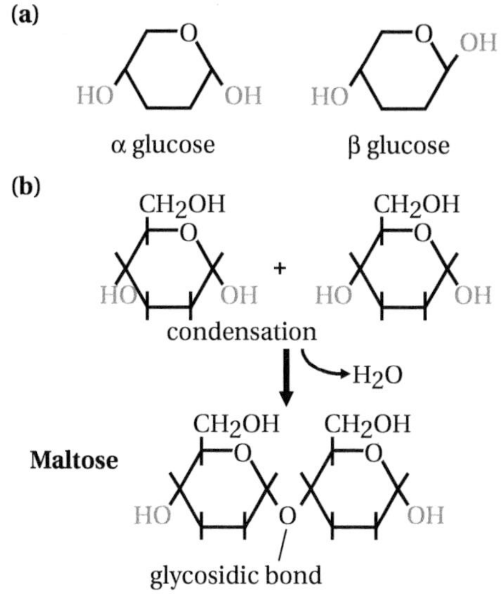

(a) α glucose β glucose

(b) condensation $\rightarrow H_2O$

Maltose

glycosidic bond

Fig 2
(a) The structure of α and β glucose
(b) Two α glucose molecules combine by condensation to form maltose. This reaction is repeated many times to form polysaccharides.

Notes

Practise drawing the formation of maltose from two glucose molecules, and make sure you can label the glycosidic bond.

Disaccharides

Common examples of disaccharides, or 'double sugars', are maltose, sucrose and lactose:

- **Maltose** is formed from two glucose molecules. It is common in germinating seeds, where it is produced by the breakdown of starch.
- **Sucrose** is formed from a glucose and a fructose molecule. It is the main transport carbohydrate in plants, so is found in high concentration in phloem tissue.
- **Lactose** is formed from a glucose and a galactose. It is found in the milk of virtually all mammals.

Polysaccharides

Complex carbohydrates are polymers, made up of repeating sugar, or saccharide units. They are also called polysaccharides. There are three polysaccharides you need to know about:

- **starch**
- **glycogen**
- **cellulose**

These are all polymers, formed from hundreds or thousands of glucose units. Starch and glycogen are made from α glucose while cellulose is made from β glucose.

Notes

Remember that storage molecules should ideally be large and insoluble so they do not have an osmotic effect and so that they are not able to diffuse out of storage cells.

Starch is the main storage compound in plants. Storage compounds need to be insoluble, compact and easily converted to energy. Starch is actually a mixture of two compounds, amylose and amylopectin (Fig 3). **Amylose** consists of single, unbranched chains of α glucose that form a spiral. **Amylopectin** consists of branched chains of α glucose molecules.

Amylose and amylopectin are large molecules, which means that they are insoluble in water. They do not, therefore, lower the water potential inside starch-containing cells. The spiral/branched structure of the molecules makes them very compact. The glucose in these compounds can only be released from the ends of the chain. As amylopectin has many branches, glucose can be released more quickly from this polysaccharide than from amylose. This is a classic example of relating structure to function.

Fig 3
Starch is a mixture of two compounds, amylose and amylopectin.

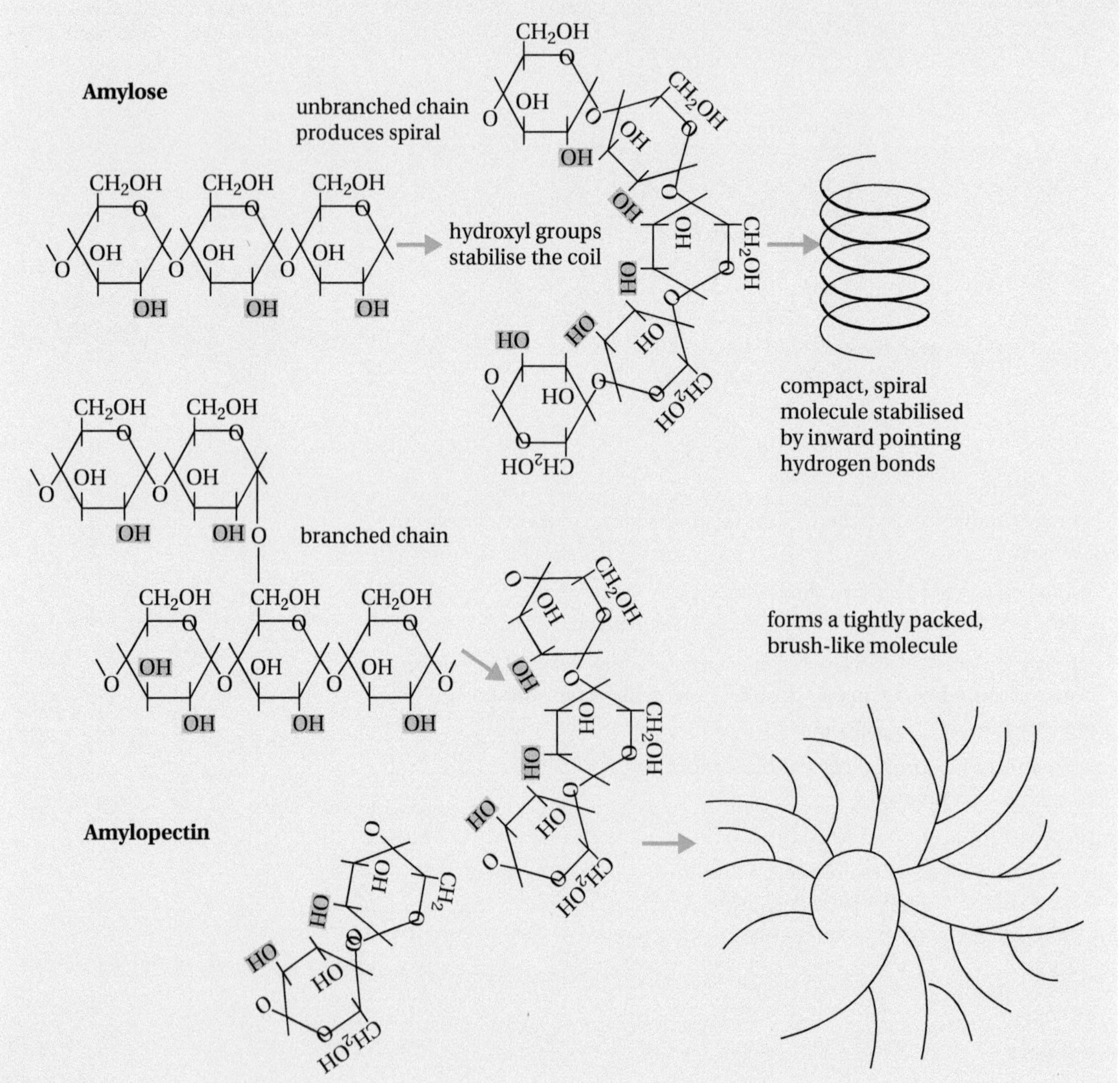

Glycogen and cellulose

Glycogen is the main storage carbohydrate in mammals. It is very similar in structure to amylopectin, but is even more branched and so can be built up and broken down even more quickly, matching the greater energy demands of animals.

Cellulose strengthens plant cell walls. It is made only from β glucose molecules (Fig 4). This slight difference in structure means that instead of forming a spiral, the β glucose chains are long and straight. When these chains lie parallel to each other, many **hydrogen bonds** form along the length so that the individual cellulose chains are bound together into strong **microfibrils.** These are then incorporated into plant **cell walls.**

Cellulose is the most abundant polysaccharide on Earth and many familiar materials, such as cotton, paper and nail varnish, owe their strength to cellulose. However, most animals cannot digest it because they do not possess the enzyme cellulase. Herbivores have microbes (bacteria and/or **protoctists**) in their guts, which do make cellulase, to help them to digest cellulose.

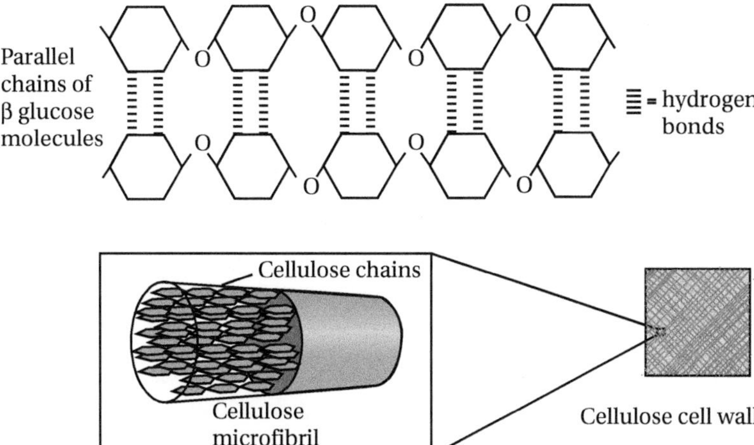

Fig 4
Cellulose consists of long parallel chains of β glucose molecules. Hydrogen bonds and other weak attractive forces all along the length bind the chains together into strong fibrils.

3.1.2.1 Biochemical tests for carbohydrates

There are several simple biochemical tests that can be used to test for the presence of different carbohydrates.

Test for a reducing sugar

Add Benedict's solution to the compound to be tested. (Note: Benedict's solution is toxic.) Heat the mixture to near boiling point in a water bath. If the compound is a reducing sugar it will reduce the *blue* copper sulphate in the Benedict's solution into *orange* copper oxide which forms a precipitate (Fig 5).

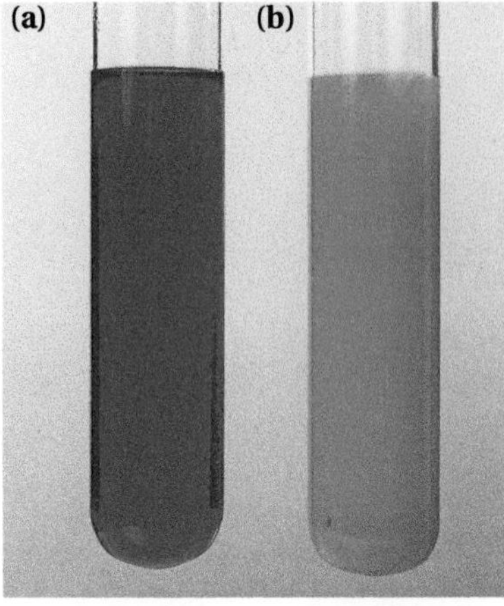

Fig 5 a and b
(a) Negative result for a reducing sugar
(b) Positive result for a reducing sugar

Notes

In questions asking for a non-reducing sugar test, you should state that you carry out the Benedict's test first to show that it is non-reducing.

Small amounts of reducing sugar will turn the mixture green and, generally, the higher the concentration of reducing sugar, the deeper the orange colour. This fact can be used to make a **quantitative** test – in other words, one that you can use to find out *how much* reducing sugar is contained in a particular sample. The amount of orange copper oxide can be compared either by filtering, drying and weighing the precipitate, or by using a **colorimeter** to estimate the depth of the orange colour (you have to compare the colour of your sample against a range of reference standards).

All the common monosaccharides (glucose, fructose and galactose) are reducing sugars, as are the disaccharides maltose and lactose. Note that sucrose is a non-reducing sugar.

Test for a non-reducing sugar

Non-reducing sugars (such as sucrose) can be detected by first boiling a sample that has previously tested negative for reducing sugar with dilute hydrochloric acid, then neutralising with sodium hydrogencarbonate. The acid hydrolyses the sugar to reducing sugars which will produce a positive result when the mixture is tested as above.

Test for starch

Add a small amount of *yellow/brown* iodine/potassium iodide solution to the compound to be tested. If starch is present a *blue/black* colour will be produced (Fig 5b). This is because the iodine fits into the spirals of the starch molecule to form a dark-coloured starch/iodine complex.

3.1.3 Lipids

Notes

Polymers consist of repeated units (monomers) joined to each other. Lipids are not polymers.

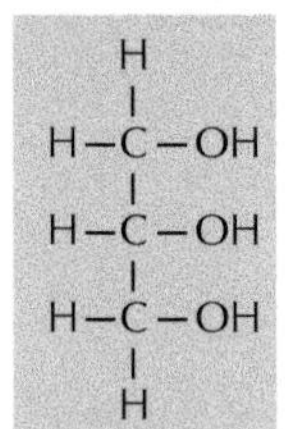

Fig 6
The structure of glycerol

Fig 7
The structure of a short chain fatty acid

Lipids are a group of compounds that includes fats, oils and waxes. They all contain the elements carbon, hydrogen and oxygen. Importantly, *lipids don't mix with water*. You need to know about two types of lipid: **triglycerides** (which store energy) and **phospholipids** (which form membranes).

Triglycerides are commonly known as fats and oils. Triglyceride molecules are made from one molecule of glycerol (Fig 6) linked to three **fatty acids.** Fatty acids are **organic acids** (also called carboxylic acids) and always have a -COOH group. This group combines with an -OH group of a glycerol molecule during a **condensation reaction**. Each reaction forms an **ester bond** which, like the glycosidic bond, centres around a shared oxygen atom.

The hydrocarbon chain of a fatty acid contains between four and 22 carbon atoms. The fatty acids shown in Figs 7 and 8 are all **saturated**, which means they are saturated with hydrogen. **Unsaturated** fatty acids may have one C=C bond that can react with hydrogen to make saturated fatty acids. **Polyunsaturated** fatty acids have more than one C=C bond. Lipids that contain saturated fatty acids are usually solid at room temperature (fats), and those containing unsaturated fatty acids are usually liquid (oils).

Triglycerides store energy: they can be respired to release more than twice as much energy as an equivalent mass of carbohydrate or protein. Other functions

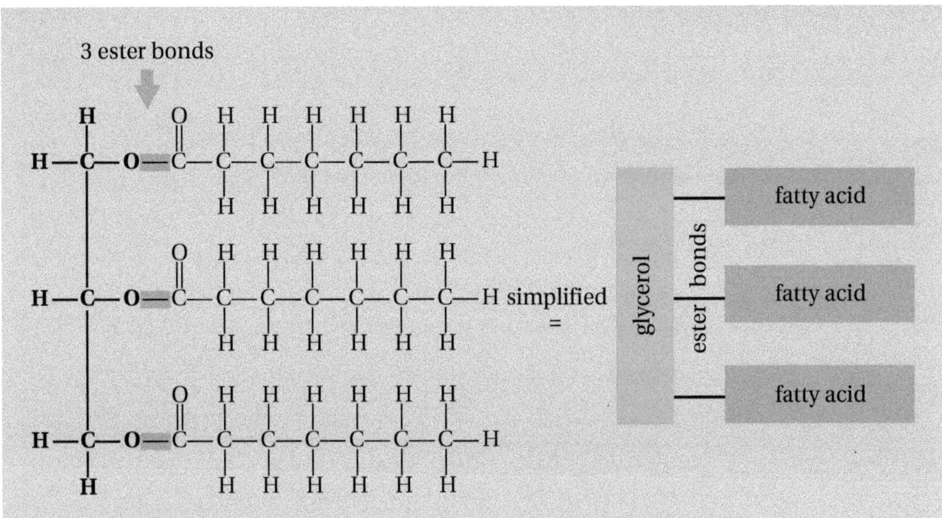

Fig 8
Three fatty acids combine with glycerol to form a triglyceride. Note the ester bonds

include insulation from the cold (for example, blubber in aquatic mammals) and protection of vital organs (for example, kidneys) from physical damage.

Lipids do not dissolve in water but they will dissolve in solvents such as ethanol. The emulsion test for lipids consists of adding ethanol to the sample and shaking it so that the lipid dissolves. The mixture is then poured into water. If the original sample contained lipid, a white emulsion (a suspension of fine droplets, like milk) will be produced.

Notes

Fatty acids really are acidic and will therefore cause a lowering in pH when they are released during digestion (hydrolysis).

Phospholipids

Phospholipids are vital in biology because they form membranes, such as the cell membrane (Fig 9). A phospholipid molecule is similar to a triglyceride except that one fatty acid is replaced by a phosphate group.

The phosphate group is highly **polar** (it carries a charge) and so attracts water molecules: in other words, it is **hydrophilic**. The fatty acid chains are not polar and so repel water, in other words, they are **hydrophobic**. So, in water, phospholipid molecules arrange themselves into structures such as micelles (spheres) and double layers (as in membranes), the hydrophilic parts pointing outwards and the hydrophobic tails pointing inwards. This automatic formation of membranes was essential to the evolution of life because it meant that the conditions inside a cell could be different to those outside.

Notes

Practise drawing the structure of fatty acids and glycerol, and the way they combine to make a triglyceride. Make sure you can label the ester bonds, and don't forget that three water molecules are made in the process.

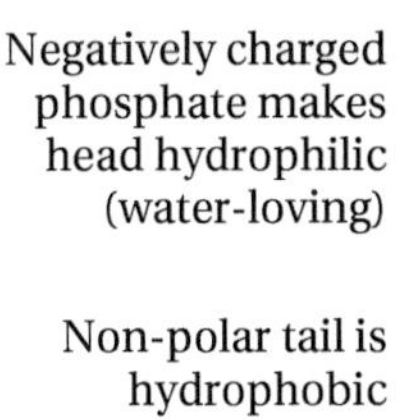

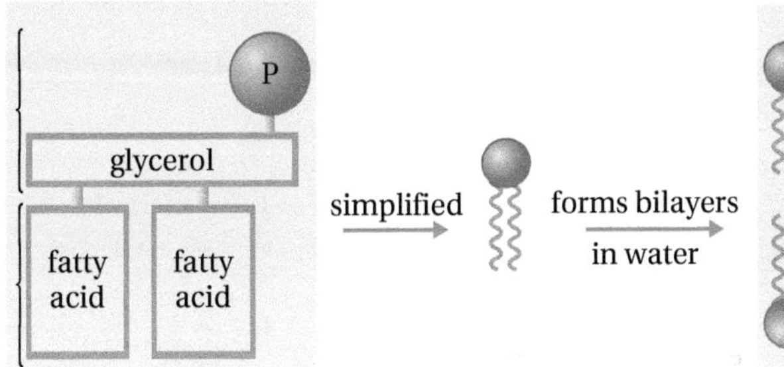

Fig 9
The structure of a phospholipid. The structure can be simplified into a sphere with two tails (often used in cell membrane diagrams).

3.1.4 Proteins

3.1.4.1 General properties of proteins

Proteins are very important in living things and the human body is no exception:

- Proteins called **enzymes** control metabolism (body chemistry) – there is a different enzyme for every reaction.
- **Antibodies** are proteins that are a vital part of the immune system.
- **Actin** and **myosin** bring about muscle contraction.
- **Collagen** gives strength to connective tissues. Tendons, cartilage and bone all owe their strength to collagen.
- Many different proteins are involved in blood clotting.
- **Keratin** is the protein that gives strength to hair, skin and nails.
- Proteins in cell membranes are vital in cell transport and **cell recognition.** Each human cell has a unique combination of proteins and other chemicals on its surface – this is why organ transplants are rejected unless careful matching is done.

A huge variety of different proteins perform all these functions. The function of an individual protein depends on its structure.

The structure of proteins

Proteins contain the elements carbon, hydrogen, oxygen and nitrogen. They often also contain sulphur.

Proteins are made up from sub-units called amino acids (Fig 10). There are 20 different amino acids. The fact that amino acids can be joined in any order to form an infinite number of different protein molecules is the key to why there is such a large variety of proteins.

Two amino acids join together in a **condensation** reaction to form a **dipeptide** (Fig 11). A chain of amino acids is known as a **polypeptide**. A protein may consist of one or more polypeptides.

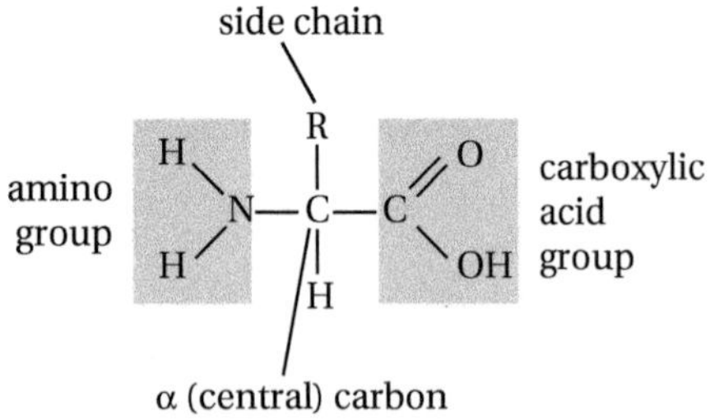

Fig 10
The basic structure of an amino acid. It's one of the basic molecules that you need to know.

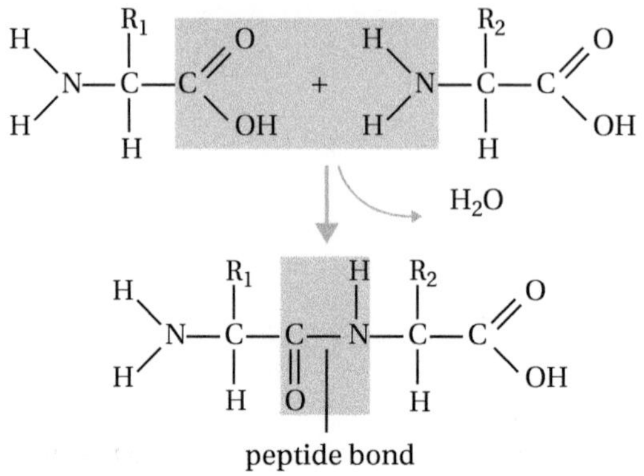

Fig 11
The formation of a dipeptide from two amino acids by a condensation reaction. Amino acids always join in the same way: the amino group of one amino acid joins with the acid group of another ('nose to tail'). So, if there is an NH_2 group at one end of the chain, there will be a -COOH group at the other.

Essential Notes

As there are 20 different amino acids, there can be 20 × 20 = 400 different dipeptides. Proteins consist of hundreds, or even thousands, of amino acids, so the number of different ones is practically infinite. Put simply, there is a great variety of proteins because there are many different building blocks.

Notes

Chromatography is a technique that separates out and identifies the components of a mixture. Paper chromatography separates out components of a mixture according to their solubility in a particular solvent. Mixtures of amino acids, or mixtures of monosaccharides are commonly separated in this way.

Proteins can be divided into two groups. Globular **proteins** such as enzymes, are roughly spherical, individual molecules that usually have a chemical function in organisms. In other words, they take part in a particular reaction. Fibrous **proteins**, which include collagen and keratin, have a structural role, such as giving strength or elasticity to a particular tissue.

The structure of proteins is complex and can be studied on four levels:

- primary
- secondary
- tertiary
- quaternary.

The **primary structure** is the sequence of amino acids in the polypeptide. An example would be alanine-glycine-leucine-valine-glutamic acid.

The **secondary structure** is the shape formed by the amino acid chain when the amino acids bend and twist to form the most stable arrangement. The commonest secondary structure is the **α helix** - a spiral shape. The **β pleated sheet** is another common secondary structure. Different regions of a polypeptide chain will have different forms of secondary structure within them (Fig 12).

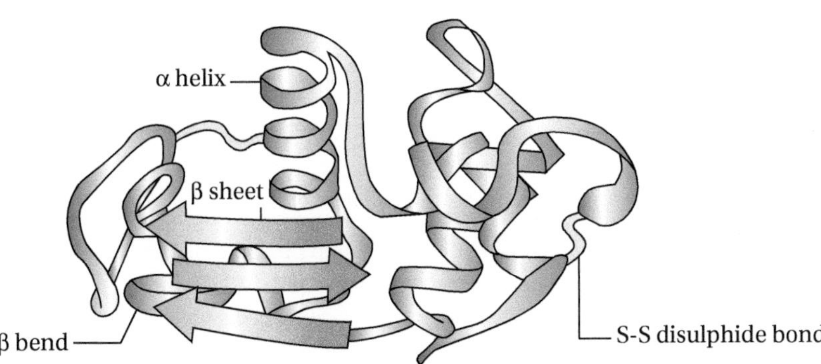

Fig 12
The tertiary structure of the protein lysozyme, an anti-bacterial compound that is present in secretions such as tears and sweat. The secondary structure is illustrated by showing α helices as spiral ribbons and β pleated sheets as broad flat arrows. You can see that there are different regions of secondary structure within the overall (tertiary) structure. Strong disulphide bonds help to maintain the shape.

The **tertiary structure** is the overall shape of the polypeptide chain (Fig 12). When a polypeptide chain bends or folds back on itself, weak **hydrogen bonds** between polar R-groups form and that stabilise the whole molecule. **Ionic bonds** between charged R-groups are slightly stronger bonds that also act to maintain the tertiary structure of the polypeptide. **Disulphide bridges** are strong bonds that can form between two sulphur-containing amino acids.

If the protein consists of only one polypeptide, the tertiary structure is the overall shape of the molecule. Some proteins consist of more than one polypeptide, in which case the **quaternary structure** is the shape created when the different polypeptide chains bind together to form the whole molecule. Insulin, for example, consists of two polypeptides; haemoglobin consists of four.

The shape of a globular protein is absolutely vital to its function. An enzyme, for instance, must have a precise tertiary and quaternary structure, otherwise it will not work. High temperature will make the molecule vibrate, breaking the weak bonds and changing the shape of the protein. This process is known as **denaturation** and it prevents the protein functioning properly. Extremes of pH can also cause denaturation.

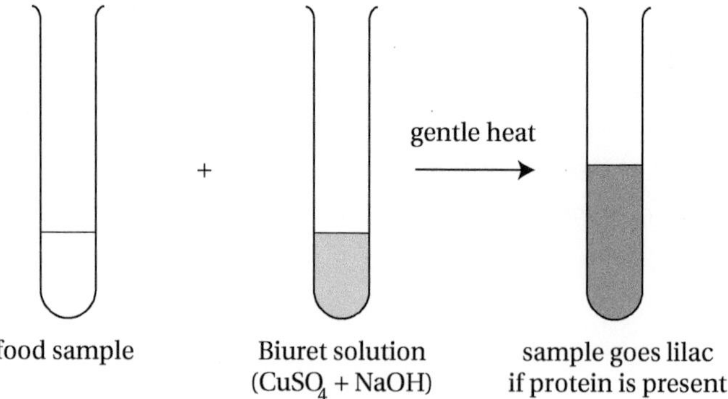

Fig 13
The Biuret test for proteins. Add a few drops of Biuret solution (a light blue compound containing copper sulphate and sodium hydroxide) to the sample to be tested. If the sample contains protein the solution will turn *lilac* (pale purple). The reaction can be speeded up by heating gently. (Note: Biuret solution is corrosive.)

3.1.4.2 Many proteins are enzymes

Some important facts you need to remember about enzymes:

- Enzymes control the rate of all metabolic reactions. The term **metabolism** refers to the many inter-related chemical reactions that take place inside an organism. This is an incredibly complex system that must be controlled, so enzymes have a vital function.
- Enzymes are proteins. They are usually named by adding the suffix '-ase' to the name of the **substrate** and/or the type of reaction being catalysed. For example, alcohol dehydrogenase removes a hydrogen atom from alcohol; **sucrase** breaks down sucrose.
- Enzymes are **catalysts**. This means that they speed up reactions and are not used up by the reactions they catalyse.

A chemical reaction will not happen unless it has enough **activation energy**. In industrial processes, activation energy is often provided as heat but living organisms cannot create or survive very high temperatures. Enzymes speed up reactions by splitting up the reaction pathway into small steps that require less energy. This enables the overall reaction to take place more easily and at lower temperatures.

Essential Notes

Activation energy is the energy needed to break existing bonds before new bonds can form.

Each enzyme has a pocket or groove in the enzyme surface that is called the **active site**. This is the exact shape to match up precisely with the substrate (Fig 14). It should be obvious, therefore, that there can only be one enzyme for each reaction: enzymes are specific.

As the reaction starts, the substrate binds momentarily to the active site of the enzyme to form an **enzyme–substrate complex**. The substrate is then transformed into product. This model of enzyme action is the **lock and key hypothesis** – only one substrate (the key) will fit into the active site (the lock). It is now thought that the active site changes shape so that the enzyme moulds itself around the substrate: this modification of the lock and key idea is known as the **induced fit hypothesis**.

Notes

DO NOT describe the active site and the substrate as the SAME SHAPE. They are complementary.

(a)

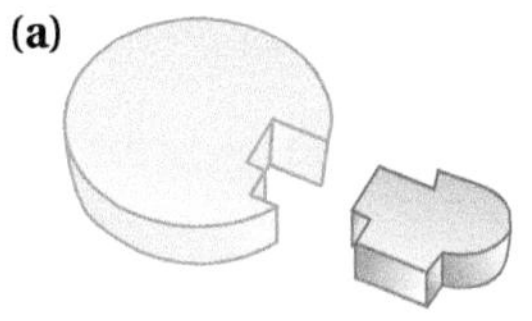

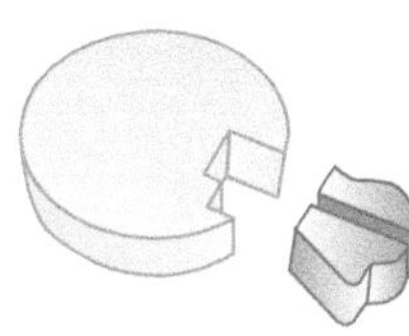

Enzyme + substrate Enzyme + substrate complex Enzyme + products

(b)

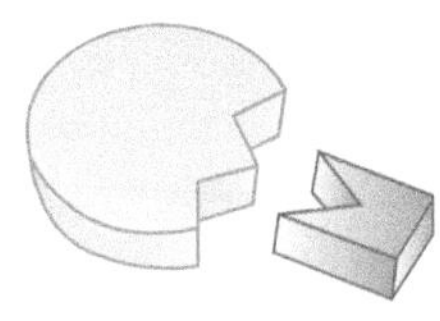

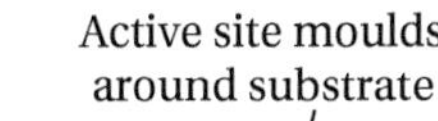

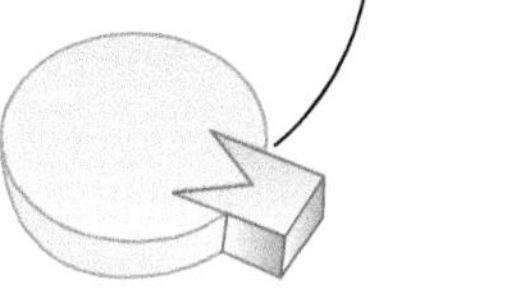

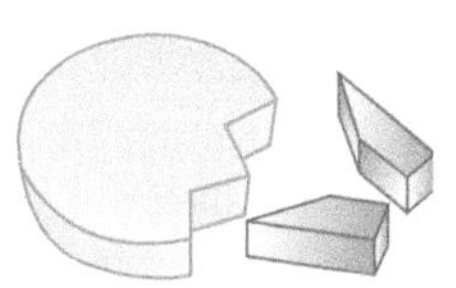

Enzyme + substrate Enzyme + substrate complex Enzyme + products

Fig 14
(a) The lock and key hypothesis – the substrate and active site are complementary in terms of shape and chemical charges.

(b) The induced fit hypothesis – as the substrate combines with the active site, the enzyme molecule alters its shape and moulds itself around the substrate.

Essential Notes

The **turnover number** is the number of substrate molecules turned into product per minute by one molecule of enzyme. It gives a measure of the speed of enzyme action. A typical value would be 200 000.

Enzyme properties

The properties of enzymes reflect the fact that they are proteins. Enzymes have a precise but delicate tertiary structure. Anything that disrupts this structure (such as high temperature or pH) or that affects the rate of formation of the enzyme–substrate complex (for example, by blocking the active site) will interfere with enzyme activity.

Notes

The fact that enzymes are proteins is a key idea for examinations, so make sure that you are familiar with the biochemistry of proteins (pages 10–11).

Rate of reaction

The rate of reaction is simply the amount of product formed (a value from the y axis) in a given time (taken from the x axis). You can think of these two values as two sides of a right-angled triangle, with the gradient of the third side being the rate. The rate is the change in y divided by the change in x.

By definition, the initial rate of reaction is taken from $t = 0$. When the graph is a curve, as is often the case, the initial rate of reaction can be calculated by simply carrying on a straight line from time 0, as shown in Fig 15. This is triangle A.

$$\text{So, initial rate of reaction} = \frac{\text{change in } y}{\text{change in } x} = \frac{(28 - 0)}{(8 - 0)}$$

$$= \frac{28}{8}$$

$$= 3.5 \text{ mol sec}^{-1}$$

Fig 15
Calculating the initial rate of a reaction

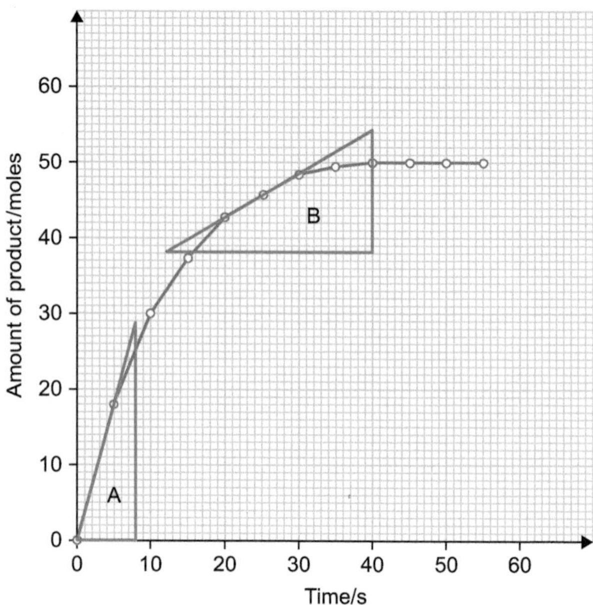

Taking it a step further, the rate of reaction at any one point can be found out by calculating the gradient of a tangent to the curve at exactly the time you want. There is an element of estimation about this; you need to draw the line so the gap between it and the curve are as equal as possible on either side of the point.

For example, if you are asked to calculate the rate at 25 seconds, draw a tangent to the curve at 25 s and construct a triangle, like example B on the diagram.

So, rate of reaction at 25 seconds $= \dfrac{\text{change in } y}{\text{change in } x}$

$$= \frac{(54 - 38)}{(40 - 13)}$$

$$= \frac{16}{27}$$

$$= 0.59 \text{ mol sec}^{-1}$$

If we want to analyse how the rate is changing with time, we can divide the rate at A by the rate at B; we get 3.5/0.59, which is 5.9 (or a ratio of 5.9:1). So, we can say that the initial rate of reaction is 5.9 times faster than it is at 25 seconds. This is probably due the substrate being used up.

Temperature

As temperature increases, so does the rate of reaction up to a critical temperature at which the enzyme becomes denatured (Fig 16). Increasing temperature gives molecules more kinetic energy, so there are more collisions. This means that more enzyme-substrate complexes form, so the rate of reaction increases. At higher temperatures, however, the enzyme molecule vibrates so much that the weak bonds maintaining the tertiary structure are broken, the shape of the molecule changes and the enzyme can no longer work. At this point the enzyme is said to be **denatured**. The temperature at which this happens varies from enzyme to enzyme, but typically it is between 50 and 60 °C.

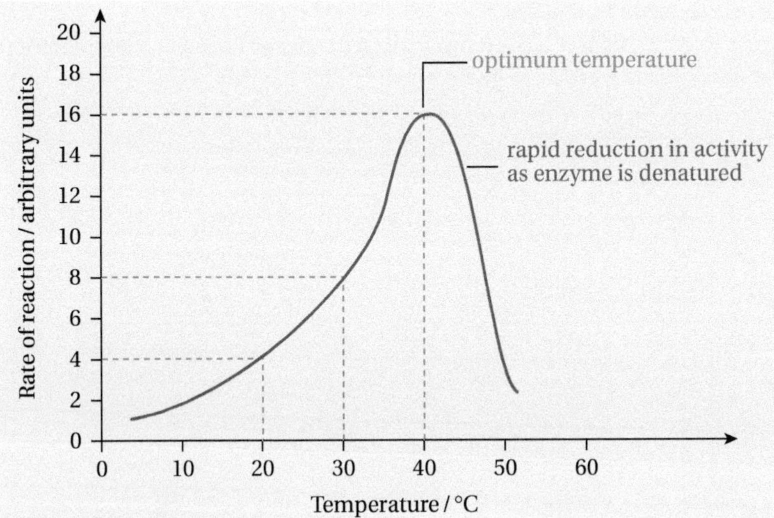

Notes

If you are given data for enzymes that are active at higher temperatures, believe the data and explain them in terms of some proteins having stronger tertiary/ quaternary bonding.

Fig 16
The relationship between enzyme activity and temperature

Essential Notes

The faster a substrate molecule moves the more likely it is to hit an active site.

Essential Notes

Thermophilic bacteria have **thermostable** enzymes that are not easily denatured. This enables them to survive at temperatures of up to 100 °C, for example, in hot volcanic springs or in deep ocean geothermal vents.

Notes

In questions on substrate or enzyme concentration, the rate of reaction is shown by the gradient of the curve (steeper = faster reaction). When the graph levels off there must be another limiting factor.

pH

The formation of the enzyme-substrate complex depends on a precise match of shape and charge. If there is a change in pH, this can cause a change in the amount of free H^+ or OH^- ions, which can disrupt these charges. All enzymes have an optimum pH. Enzymes that work inside cells (intracellular) usually work best at a pH of 7.3–7.45 (Fig 17). Some extracellular enzymes, such as the digestive enzymes of the stomach and small intestine, work best at extremes of pH.

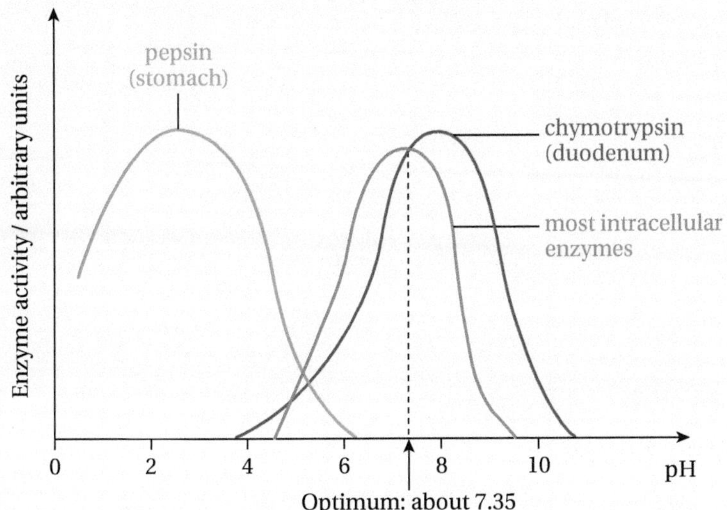

Fig 17
Graph showing the effect of pH on enzyme activity

Notes

In exam answers, always try to use scientific language. In enzyme questions, examiners expect to see words such as *collisions, enzyme–substrate complexes, tertiary structure, active site and denatured.*

Notes

Be careful not to refer to an enzyme's active site as being 'used up'.

Substrate concentration

The greater the substrate concentration, the faster the rate of reaction until the enzymes are working as fast as possible. This happens when *all* active sites are filled *all* the time (Fig 18). At this point the rate of reaction can only be increased further by adding more enzyme.

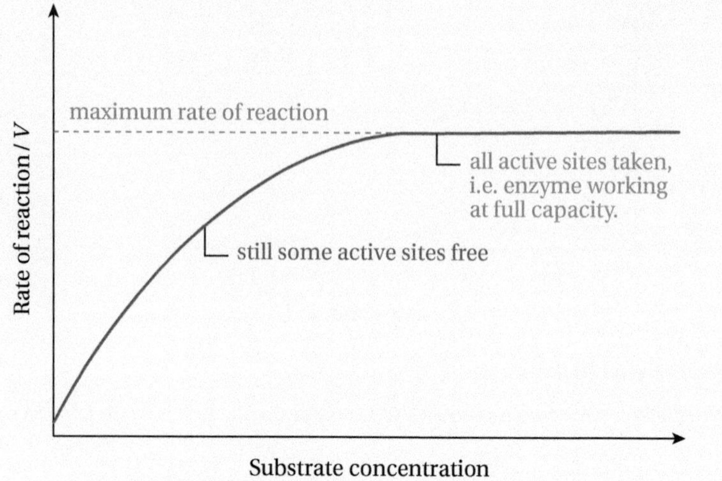

Fig 18
The relationship between substrate concentration and rate of reaction

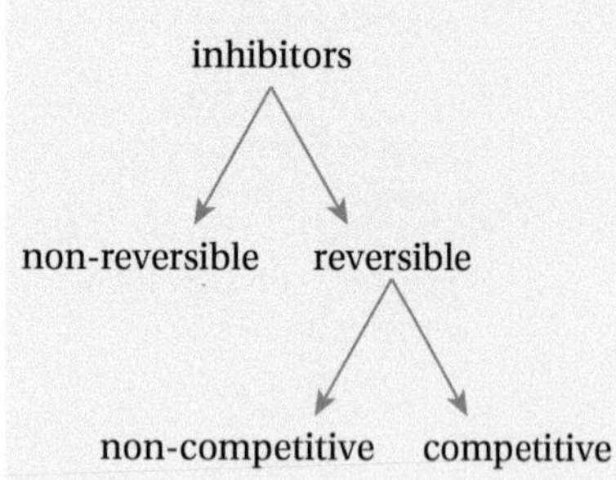

Fig 19
Simple overview of inhibition

The effect of enzyme concentration

In a similar way to substrate concentration, the higher the enzyme concentration, the greater the rate of reaction, until the amount of substrate becomes a limiting factor.

Inhibition of enzymes

An **inhibitor** is a substance that slows down or stops enzyme action (Fig 19). Most reactions with inhibitors are *reversible*, which means that they do not combine with the enzyme molecule permanently. There are two types of reversible inhibitor, **competitive inhibitors** and **non-competitive inhibitors**.

Fig 20
The effect of a competitive inhibitor on enzyme activity

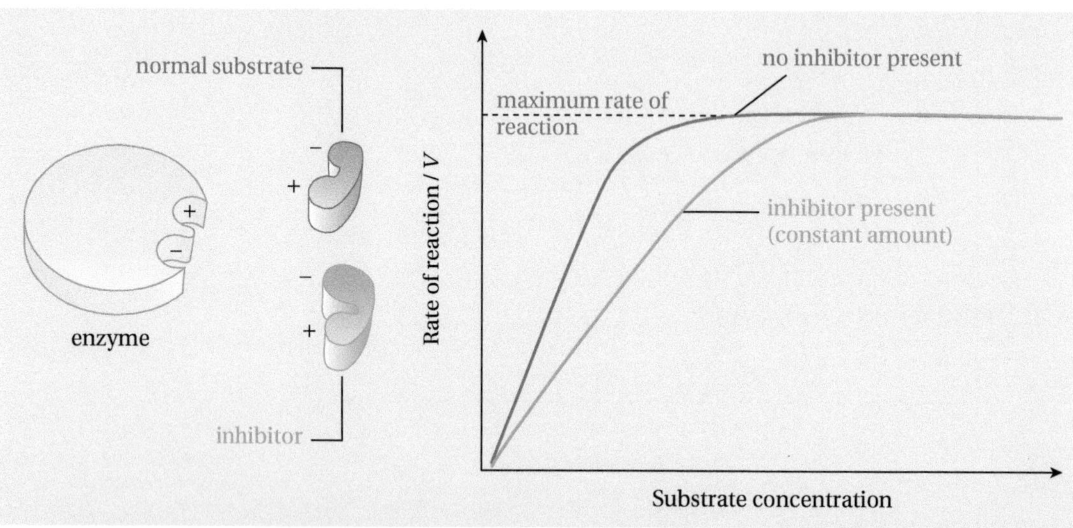

Competitive inhibitors are very similar to the substrate in terms of their 3D shape. This allows them to enter the active site and effectively 'get in the way' so that the substrate cannot enter (Fig 20). They compete with the substrate for the active site. If more substrate is added, the effect of the inhibitor will be reduced.

Non-competitive inhibitors bind to the enzyme molecule at a position away from the active site, but they change the tertiary structure. This modifies the shape of the active site so that the enzyme–substrate complex cannot form. In this case adding more substrate will have no effect on the rate of reaction, or on the level of inhibition (Fig 21).

Fig 21
The effect of a non-competitive inhibitor on enzyme activity

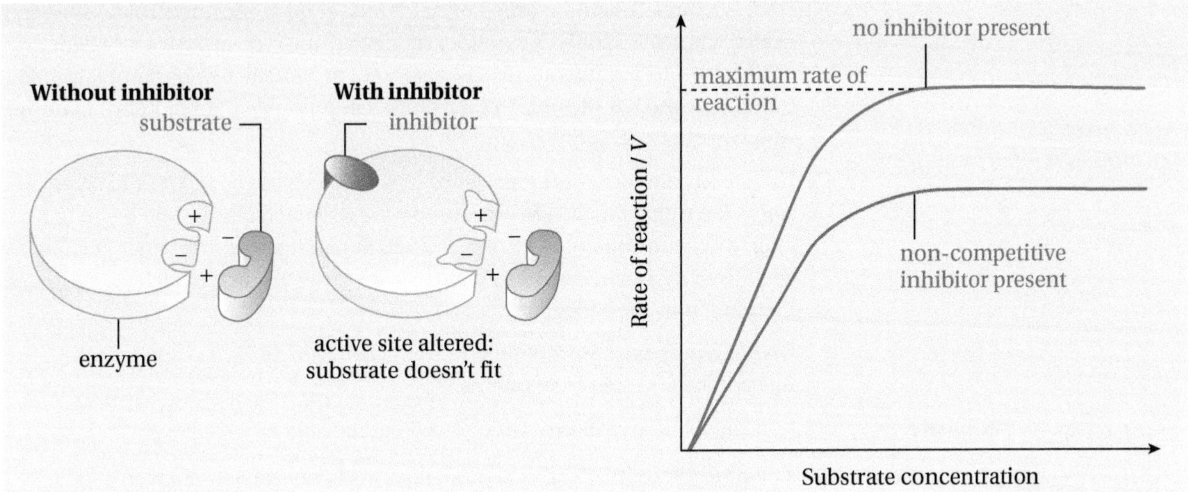

Essential Notes

Metabolism in living cells is largely controlled by non-competitive inhibitors that temporarily deactivate enzymes when their product is not needed. As a general idea, hormones work by switching enzymes and enzyme systems on or off. Think of enzymes as workers and hormones as bosses.

Our understanding of enzyme action

Our understanding of how enzymes work changes as technology improves. The lock and key model has largely been replaced by the 'induced fit' model. Evidence for induced fit includes the fact that non-competitive inhibitors can change the shape of an enzyme to an inactive form, showing that the shape of the enzyme molecule is not fixed. The precise 3D shape of enzymes can be modelled on a computer, where the sequence of amino acids can be used to predict the tertiary structure, including where and how the molecule will be flexible.

3.1.5 Nucleic acids are important information-carrying molecules

3.1.5.1 Structure of DNA and RNA

DNA is a remarkable molecule with two key abilities:

- It carries information – the **genetic code** – from which the essential proteins are made. This process is called protein synthesis.
- It can make exact copies of itself, time after time. This process is called **DNA replication**. Without this ability there would be no cell division and therefore no growth, repair or reproduction.

DNA is a **nucleic acid**, so called because it is found in the nucleus and is weakly acidic. It is a stable **polynucleotide**: stable because it does not start to denature until heated to a temperature of about 90 °C; polynucleotide because it is made from many **nucleotide** units. DNA is much more stable than proteins, many of which begin to denature around 40–50 °C.

DNA molecules are enormous – the largest molecules you are ever likely to study. If a single human **chromosome** were stretched out it could be up to 5 cm long, when most molecules are measured in nanometres. Obviously DNA never gets stretched out because it remains locked away inside the nucleus, and therefore must be coiled up.

DNA is a **polymer**: the monomers are nucleotides. As Fig 22 shows, each nucleotide has three components:

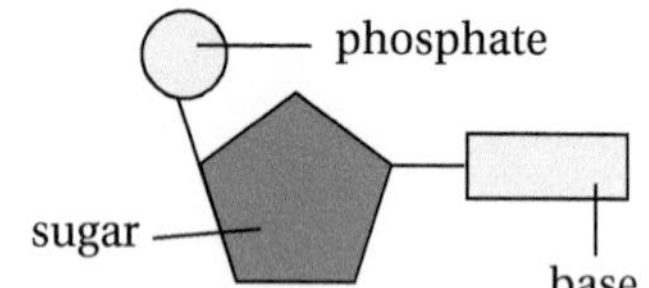

Fig 22
The basic structure of a nucleotide

- a **sugar** – deoxyribose – which is a 5-carbon sugar
- a **phosphate** (PO_4^{3-}) group (note that this is a negatively charged phosphate **ion**)
- a **base** – one of four nitrogen-containing compounds – adenine (A), thymine (T), guanine (G) or cytosine (C).

The nucleotides are arranged in a double helix – a twisted ladder. The two sides of the ladder are chains of alternating sugar-phosphate groups, while the 'rungs' are made from pairs of bases bonded together by hydrogen bonds. For both protein synthesis and **replication**, it is important that the strands can separate and rejoin without damaging the molecule. Only one part of one strand of the DNA at any particular point in the double-stranded molecule – the **sense strand** – is used to make proteins. The other side serves to stabilise the molecule. The sense strand for different genes may be found on different sides of the molecule.

The sugar in one nucleotide is joined to the phosphate of the next nucleotide by phosphodiester bonds. These strong, covalent bonds are important in the stability of the DNA molecule. H bonds are easily broken (chemists say that H bonds are 'overcome' rather than broken) but the phosphodiester bonds are not.

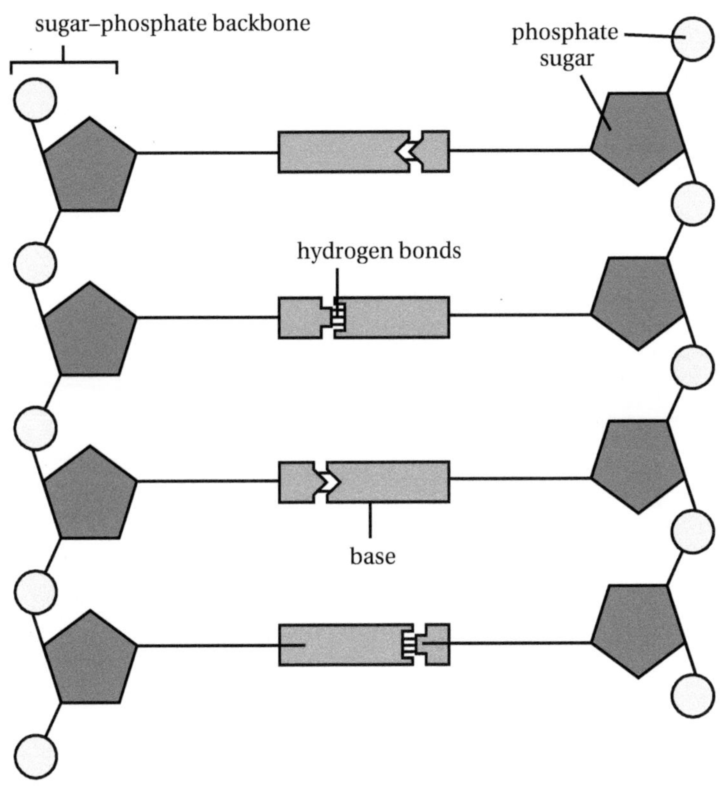

Fig 23
Nucleotides are joined by condensation reactions to form a single DNA chain, which bonds with a complementary DNA chain. These chains twist together to make a double helix. The covalent bonds between the sugar and phosphate groups are much stronger than hydrogen bonds.

The bases in a DNA molecule

The four bases in a DNA molecule always bond in the same way - A to T and C to G. So if you know the base sequence down one side of the DNA molecule, you can predict the sequence on the other.

For example:
If one side reads CGCGTTAATACGC
the other side will read GCGCAATTATGCG

The bases are held together by hydrogen bonds, two between A and T (A=T) and three between C and G (G≡C). These regular hydrogen bonds along the whole length of the molecule make DNA very stable.

Notes
Practise predicting the sequence of bases along a strand of DNA from the sequence on the opposite strand.

3.1.5.2 DNA replication

The existence of a molecule that can store information and copy itself is essential to life. If this did not happen, characteristics could not be passed on from generation to generation. But how does DNA copy itself?

In DNA replication the two strands come apart, and each one acts as a template for the addition of complementary nucleotides (Fig 24).

The basic process of replication involves these steps:

1 **Helicase** enzymes unwind the two strands of the DNA helix, breaking the hydrogen bonds and separating the two strands.
2 DNA binding proteins attach to keep the strands apart.

3 Primase enzymes add **primers**; short sections of nucleotides that signal to the polymerase enzyme where to begin copying.

4 **DNA polymerase** enzymes attach to the primers and then move along the exposed strands, catalysing the addition of complementary nucleotides to complete the new strands.

5 Mistakes do occur, when the wrong base is inserted, but most of them are corrected by **proofreading** enzymes. Those that are not corrected can lead to mutations.

DNA replication is **semi-conservative** because in each daughter DNA molecule one strand is original (it has been conserved) and the other strand is new.

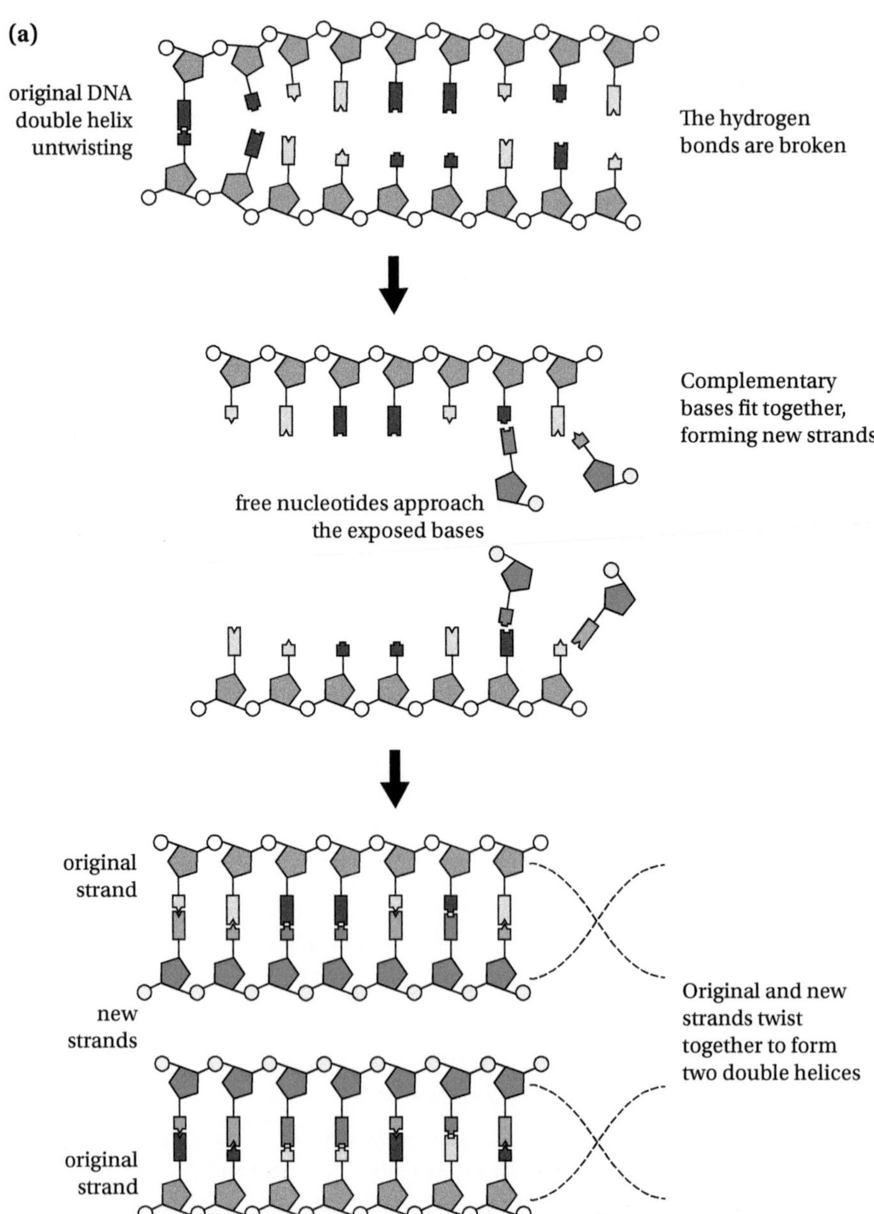

Fig 24a
The process of DNA replication

Evidence for the semi-conservative theory of DNA replication

Strong support for the idea that DNA replication is semi-conservative came from a series of classic experiments performed by Meselson and Stahl in the 1950s.

They used an isotope of nitrogen, ^{15}N (heavy nitrogen), that can be incorporated into DNA instead of the normal isotope, ^{14}N, without harming the organism. However, this makes the DNA slightly denser and so DNA containing ^{14}N can be separated from that containing ^{15}N by centrifugation (Fig 25, page 22). In this way they were able to show that each new DNA molecule contains one original strand and one new strand.

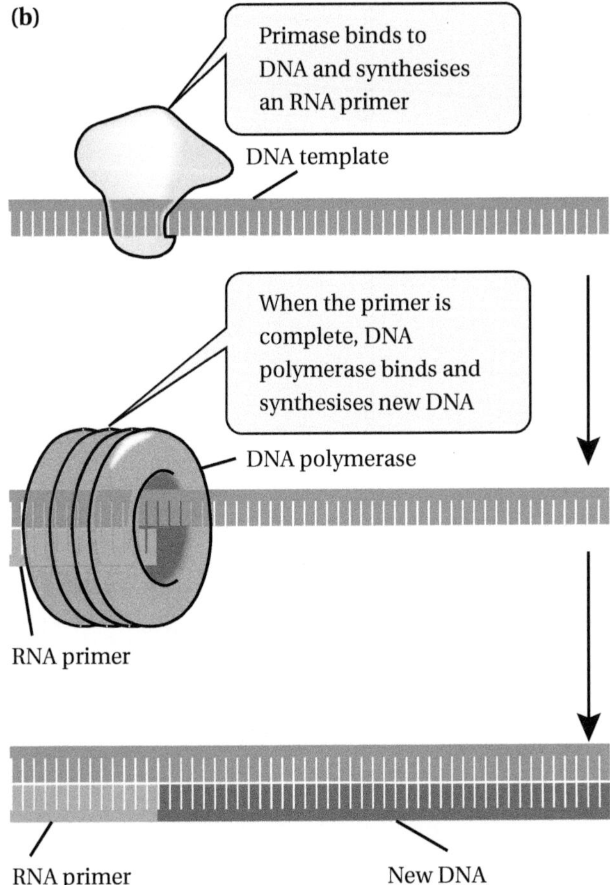

Fig 24b
DNA replication showing the action of primers

You may get diagrams in which the two original 'heavy' strands are labelled, and be asked to predict what will happen next. Remember that in each of the generations that follow, there will only be two of these heavy strands.

- In generation 0 there will be one piece of DNA, which will have two heavy strands.
- In generation 1 there will be two pieces of DNA, both hybrid, so one heavy strand and one light strand.
- In generation 2 there will be four pieces of DNA, two hybrid and two all new.
- In generation 3 there will be eight pieces of DNA, two hybrid and six all new.

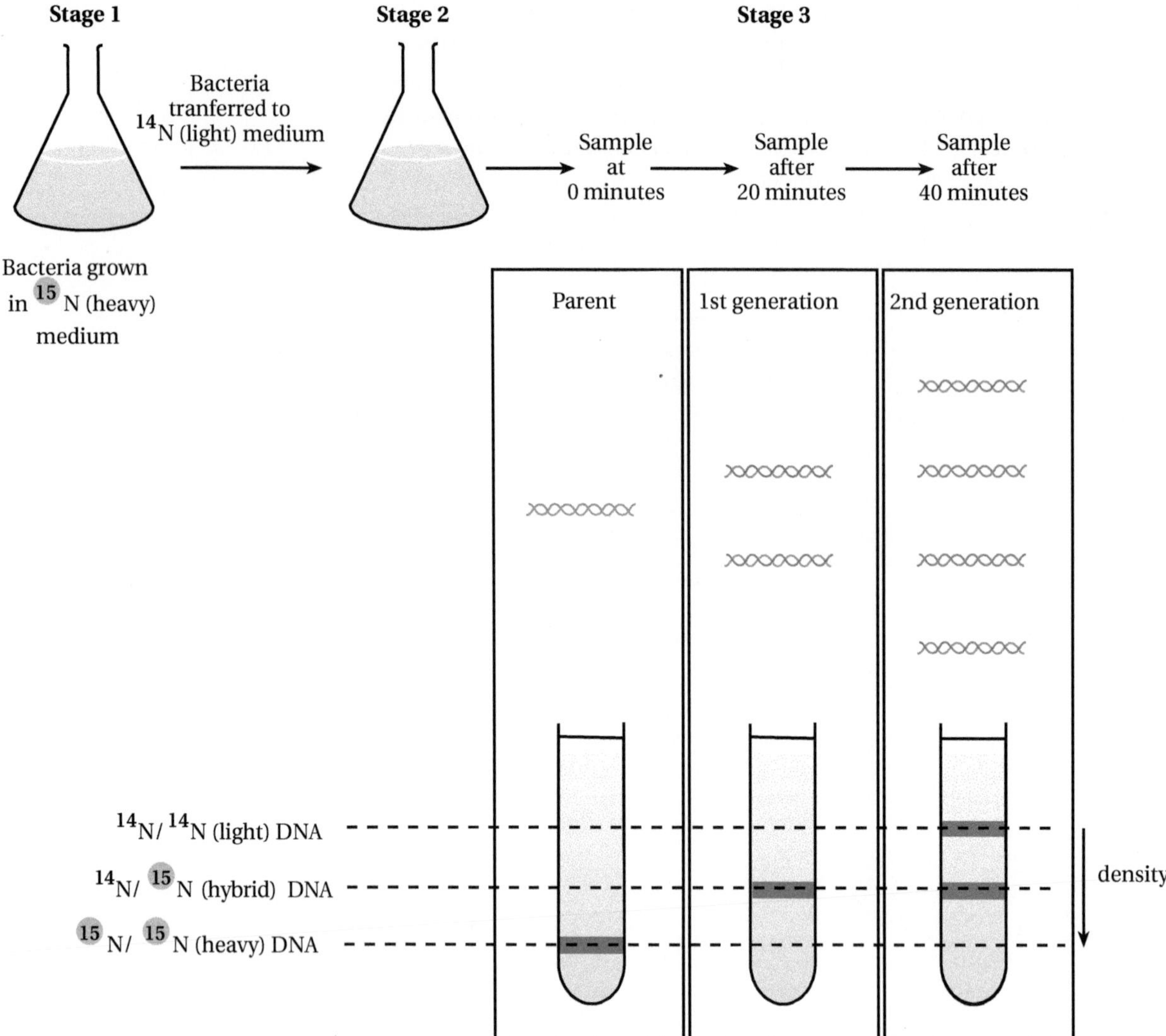

Fig 25
An outline of Meselson and Stahl's experiment.

And in each subsequent generation there will be two hybrid strands, which will eventually be far outnumbered by the all-new strands.

You might also be given diagrams of tubes. Remember that DNA with two labelled (^{15}N) strands is the heaviest, followed by DNA with one labelled strand, and DNA with no labelled strands is the lightest or least dense.

3.1.6 ATP

- **ATP** stands for adenosine triphosphate. It can be **hydrolysed** (broken down) into adenosine diphosphate (ADP) and free inorganic phosphate (P_i) (Fig 26).
- Splitting ATP provides readily available energy in small, usable amounts for the wide variety of energy-requiring reactions that occur in cells.
- ATP releases energy instantly because it is broken down in one simple chemical step: the breaking of the phosphate to phosphate bond.
- ATP is a relatively small molecule that can diffuse around the cell quickly.
- ATP is an intermediate energy source within cells. It carries energy from the site of respiration, mainly the **mitochondria**, to other areas of the cell where energy is needed.

In respiration, the energy contained in organic compounds is released in a series of steps. This energy is used to make ATP from ADP and phosphate. Respiration can therefore be thought of as a process that replenishes ATP stocks, making sure that it is made as fast as it is used.

The ATP, ADP and P_i in a cell are sometimes known as the 'phosphate battery'. If all of the phosphate were to exist as ATP, the battery would be 'fully charged'. However, ATP is an unstable molecule, and is constantly being broken down and re-synthesised in a cycle within the cell.

Notes

ATP and energy are not the same. You cannot say that ATP is energy – ATP is a molecule that releases energy when it is hydrolysed to form ADP and phosphate.

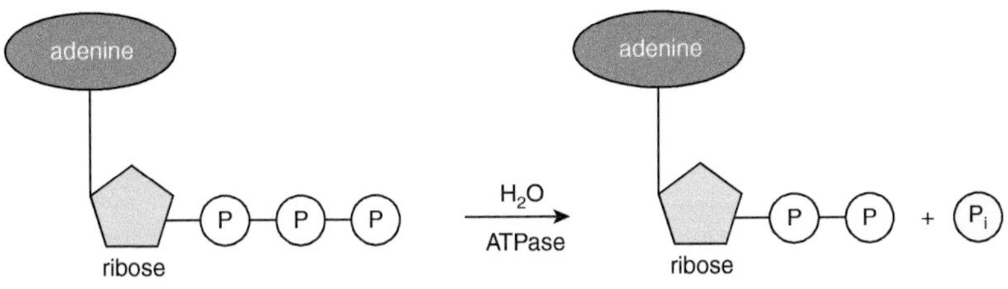

ATP ⟶ **ATP + P_i + energy**

Fig 26
The hydrolysis (splitting) of ATP. This reaction releases energy that can be used to drive energy-requiring reactions, such as muscular contraction.

3.1.7 Water

Water is a small molecule. The formula of H_2O gives it a relative molecular mass of 18 and most substances of this size are gases. However, the two pairs of electrons on the oxygen atom repel the hydrogen atoms, resulting in a **dipole**, i.e. areas of positive and negative charge. As a consequence, water molecules are **cohesive** ('sticky'): **hydrogen bonds** form between the positive and negative areas of different molecules, attracting them together and making water a liquid at most of the temperatures found on Earth.

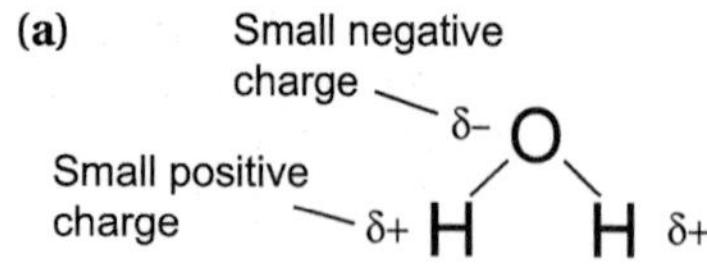

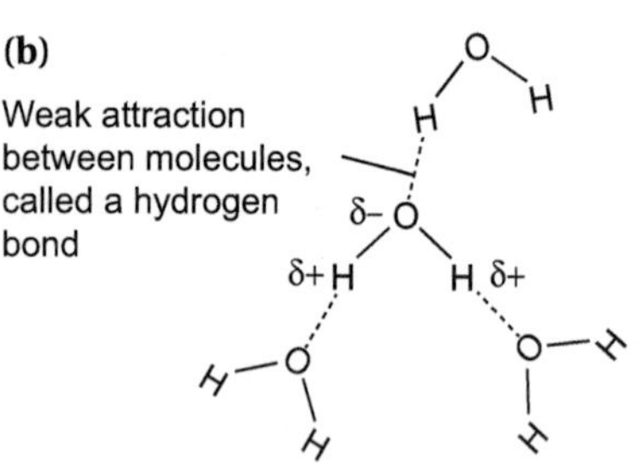

Figure 27
Hydrogen bonding attracts water molecules together. The dipole is written as δ+ and δ–. Effectively, water molecules cling to each other, or to other ions and molecules that have a positive or negative charge.

Life cannot exist without liquid water. All active, living cells contain water. They are also surrounded by water, whether they are free-living microbes or part of a large multicellular organism. As a result, search for extraterrestrial life centres around identifying planets that might contain liquid water.

The hydrogen bonding gives water some very important properties:

- It is a **solvent** for all **polar molecules**, so sugars, amino acids and ions are all water soluble. In contrast, non-polar molecules will dissolve in lipids.
- It is cohesive, so forms long unbroken columns inside conducting tissue such as xylem and phloem vessels. If it wasn't this cohesive, it would be impossible to pull long columns of water up to the tops of tall trees.
- This cohesion also results in **surface tension**, at the interface of water and air. Many plants and animals take advantage of surface tension to live just under or just above the surface of water.
- It is a **metabolite** in many important reactions. Condensation reactions involve small molecules joining to form lager ones, forming water in the process. Hydrolysis is the opposite process, in which water is used to split larger molecules into smaller ones.
- It has a relatively high **specific heat capacity**, meaning that it can absorb a lot of energy before the temperature drops, and absorb a lot before it rises. As a consequence, it acts as a thermal buffer. Organisms, which are mainly water, heat up and cool down relatively slowly, as do aquatic habitats such as oceans, lakes and rivers.
- It has a high **latent heat of vaporisation**, which means that the evaporation of even a small amount of water has a relatively large cooling effect. Sweating and panting are effective cooling techniques, and transpiration from plants also has a significant cooling effect.

3.1.8 Inorganic ions

Notes

If you know the hydrogen ion concentration of a solution, you can work out its pH according to the formula pH = $-\log_{10} [H^+]$.

For example, if the concentration of H^+ ions is 1.4×10^{-5}M, pH = $-\log_{10} [1.4 \times 10^{-5}]$ (a scientific calculator will sort this out for you), and pH = 4.85.

You do not need to learn this equation.

Inorganic ions occur in solution in the cytoplasm and body fluids of organisms.

Hydrogen ions

Hydrogen ions (H^+) are simply protons. The abundance of H^+ ions determines the pH of a solution.

The control of pH is important because enzymes are very pH-sensitive. Even slight changes in pH can cause a metabolic imbalance because enzymes begin to work at different rates. Extremes of pH can denature enzymes.

The membranes of many cells have 'proton pumps' which move H^+ ions by active transport. One example of this is seen in the stomach, where proton pumps give gastric juice a pH of about 1.

Iron ions

A vital function of iron is to form the centre of haem groups in **haemoglobin**. It is the Fe^{2+} ion that actually combines with the oxygen molecule. In every haemoglobin molecule there are four haem groups and therefore four iron ions that can combine with a molecule of oxygen, giving oxyhaemoglobin, which is abbreviated to HbO_8.

> **Notes**
>
> Substances that resist pH changes are called **buffers**. Haemoglobin is an important buffer in blood, and there are several inorganic buffers in blood plasma.

Sodium ions

Sodium (Na^+) ions are the most common positive ions (cations) in the body. Sodium has a variety of important functions including the transmission of nerve impulses, the absorption of glucose and amino acids from the gut (see: co-transport) and the control of water potential (osmoregulation).

Phosphate ions

Phosphate ions (PO_4^-) ions are essential components of many important biological molecules including DNA, RNA, ATP and phospholipids.

3.2 Cells

3.2.1 Cell structure

3.2.1.1 Structure of eukaryotic cells

Typical animal cell

A good example of a typical animal cell is the epithelial cell from the small intestine (Fig 28). It is part of a tissue that lines the intestine and is adapted for the absorption of digested food. Under the light microscope these visible features are typical of most animal cells:

- The **nucleus** - a large circular structure that contains DNA.
- The **cell-surface membrane** - a very thin membrane that surrounds the cell.
- The **cytoplasm** - literally 'cell fluid'. This contains many different structures, or **organelles** (see Fig 28).

See Table 1 on pages 26 to 27 for details about cell function.

> **Notes**
>
> There is often a light micrograph and/or an electron micrograph to interpret on the exam paper – so make sure you can identify organelles in each.

Ultrastructure in eukaryotic cells

Ultrastructure means 'fine detail'. When viewed with an electron microscope, the cytoplasm of a plant or animal cell (called **eukaryotic** cells) is seen to contain many different organelles. The main ones are described in Table 1.

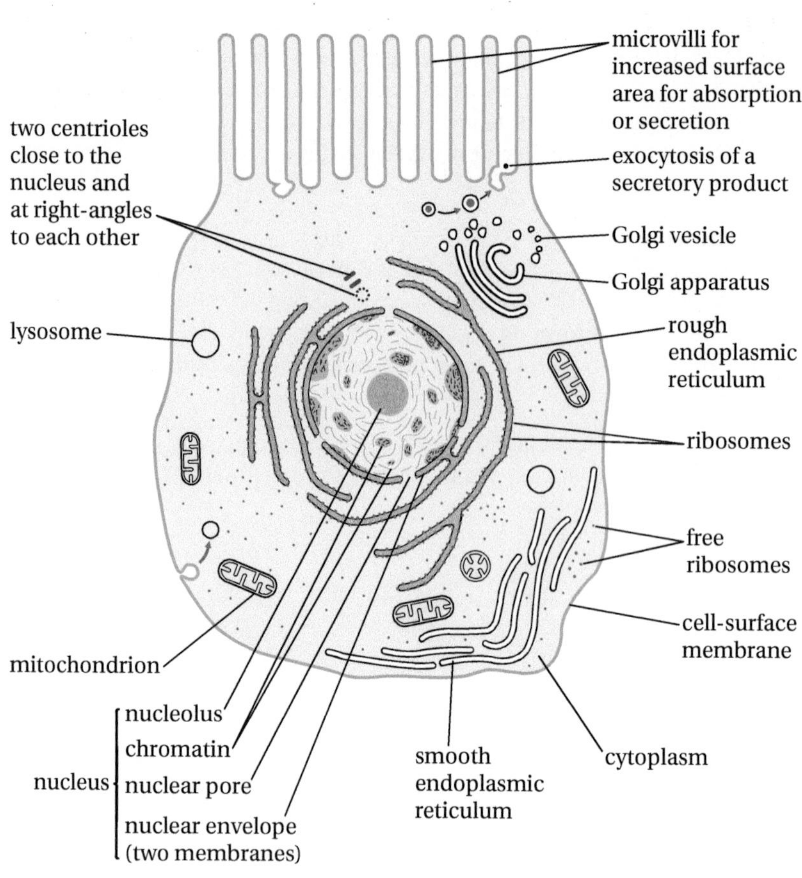

Fig 28
The epithelial cells that line the small intestine show many typical features of animal cells.

Table 1
The main eukaryotic organelles

Organelle	Diagram	Description	Size/Distribution	Function
Cell surface membrane		Thin boundary between cell and environment	Universal – it surrounds all cells in all organisms. Most organelles are surrounded by a similar membrane	Controls what passes in and out of the cell (see page 34). Similar membranes surround organelles, for example, mitochondria, nucleus. Proteins attached to the cell membrane play a part in cell recognition, for example, by the immune system and cell transport. Microvilli are folds in the membrane that increase the surface area for absorption.

Table 1 (continued)
The main eukaryotic organelles

Organelle	Diagram	Description	Size/Distribution	Function
Nucleus	nucleolus	Large, usually spherical, bounded by a double membrane with many pores	About 10 μm in diameter, usually one per cell	Contains the DNA. Key functions are replication, cell division and protein synthesis. In eukaryotic cells DNA is linear and attached to proteins (**histones**)
Mitochondrion		Usually round and elongated, smooth outer membrane, folded inner membrane	1–10 μm in size, up to 1000 in cytoplasm of each cell	Site of aerobic respiration – most of the cell's ATP is made here. The more metabolically active the cell, the more folds there are in the mitochondria
Rough endoplasmic reticulum (rough ER)		Extensive membrane system, many cavities and tubes, ribosomes attached	Throughout cytoplasm, connected to nuclear membrane	Transport system in the cytoplasm; collects, stores, packages and transports the proteins made on the ribosomes
Smooth endoplasmic reticulum (smooth ER)		Membrane system with small cavities, no ribosomes attached	Small patches in cytoplasm	Synthesis of lipids and some steroids. Detoxification, for example, alcohol breakdown
Golgi apparatus		Stack of flattened membrane discs	Size varies, found free in cytoplasm close to rough ER	Receives packages (**vesicles**) of protein from rough ER. Appears to synthesise/ modify chemicals before their secretion from cell
Ribosome	small subunit large subunit	Small and dense structure, like a giant enzyme. No membrane	Size 20 nm, attached to ER or free in cytoplasm	Site of translation: the part of the cell where the genetic code is used to build protein
Lysosome		Small vesicle (sphere) of membrane that contains digestive enzymes	Free in cytoplasm	Breakdown of substances, organelles or whole cells, for example, in phagocytosis, lysosomes are used by white cells to destroy bacteria

Plant cells

Like animal cells, plant cells have a nucleus, mitochondria, cell membrane and cytoplasm. They also have a few extra features:

- A **cell wall** – a tough layer made of cellulose, which surrounds plant cells
- A **vacuole** – a large, membrane-bound organelle, which usually contains fluid
- **Chloroplasts** – organelles that contain chlorophyll and that are the site of photosynthesis.

A typical plant cell

Palisade mesophyll cells are typical plant cells (Fig 29). They are found in leaves and are adapted for photosynthesis.

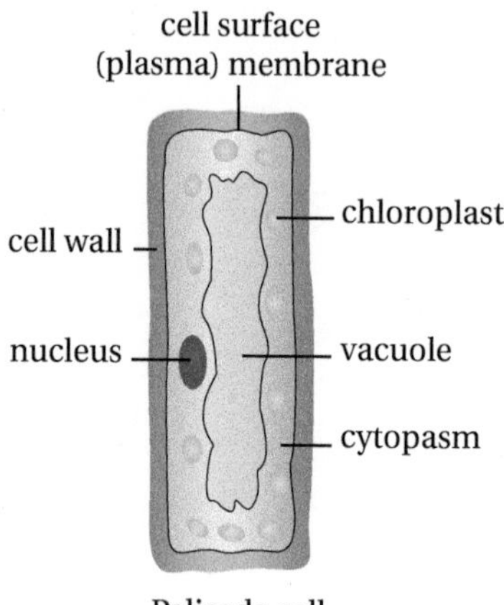

Fig 29
A palisade mesophyll cell, as seen under the optical (or light) microscope, shows many features typical of plant cells. These cells are adapted for photosynthesis and are packed with chloroplasts. Their deep, cylindrical shape means that they can be packed tightly together to maximise light absorption.

The cell wall

The cell wall is secreted by the plant cell itself. As Fig 4 shows, the long cellulose molecules are arranged into **microfibrils**, which become cemented into the cell wall using a 'glue' that consists of short chains of glucose molecules.

The wall, which resembles fibreglass when observed under the electron microscope, has several functions:

- It gives the plant cell rigidity and strength.
- It prevents the cell from swelling and bursting due to water intake. The **protoplast** inside the cell swells and pushes against the cell wall until no further expansion is possible, like a bladder in a football. In this state the cell is said to be **turgid**.
- In multicellular plants, this turgidity gives mechanical strength to the tissues.
- It gives the cell a particular shape. A good example of this is seen in **xylem** fibres (Fig 30), when the cytoplasm in the young xylem vessel dies, leaving just the cell walls to conduct water and dissolved mineral ions up the plant.

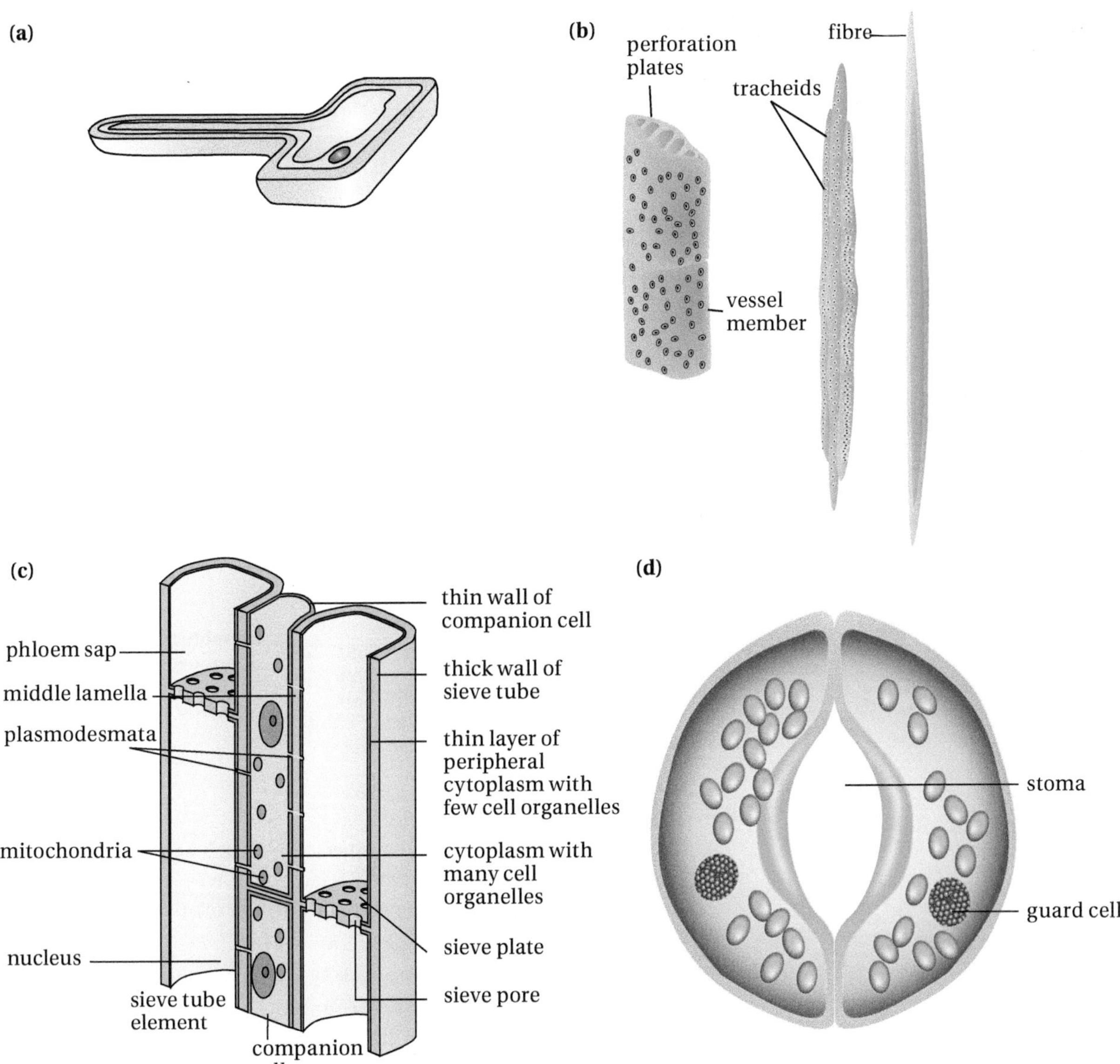

Fig 30
Some specialised plant cells
(a) Root hair cell - projects into the soil and provides a large surface area for the absorption of water and mineral ions
(b) Xylem - specialised conducting cells, with strengthened walls and hollow ends that provide a continuous pathway for water transport
(c) Phloem - transports sugars and other organic materials around the plant
(d) Guard cell - can change shape to open or close the stomata

Chloroplasts

Chloroplasts are organelles that contain all the pigments, enzymes and other substances needed for photosynthesis. They are found mainly in the palisade cells of the leaf. Fig 31 shows the ultrastructure of chloroplasts. Key features include:

- A large internal surface area so that as much chlorophyll as possible comes into contact with light
- A flattened shape to enable rapid **diffusion** of substances in and out.

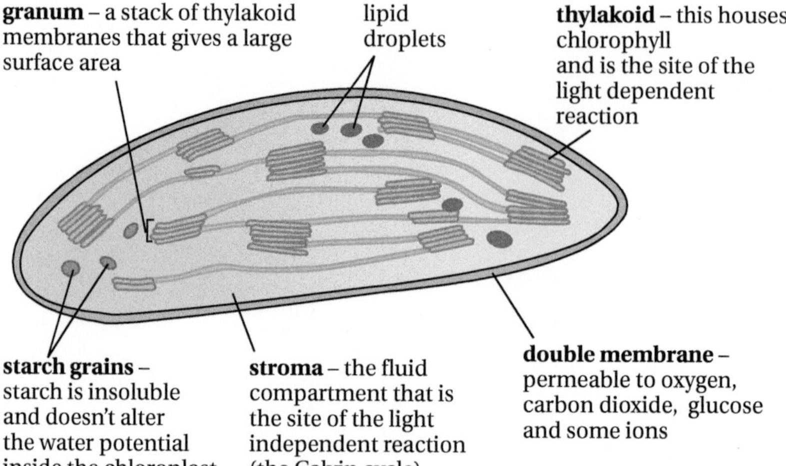

Fig 31
Chloroplasts take the form of flattened discs, rather like Smarties™ (but don't call them that in the exam)

Cells, tissues, organs and systems

In early human embryos the cells are unspecialised, but have the potential to differentiate into any of the 200 or so specialised cell types that make up the human body. The tissues and organs of the body develop because cells differentiate in the right way at the right time.

- A **tissue** is an aggregation of similar cells. The human body is made up of four basic tissue types; nerve, muscle, connective and epithelial. Within these groups there are many sub-divisions.
- **Organs** are aggregations of tissues performing specific physiological functions. For example heart, liver, kidney.
- **Systems** are groups of organs that work together to achieve a major physiological function. Examples include digestive, respiratory, nervous and circulatory.

It is not just humans that have tissues, organs and organ systems. The cells of other multicellular organisms, including plants, may differentiate and become adapted for specific functions.

Adaptations in plant cells

Some plant cells have specialised functions, and this is reflected by their structure (Fig 30).

3.2.1.2 Structure of prokaryotic cells and of viruses

Bacteria, bacterial disease and the cell membrane

Bacteria are simple, single-celled organisms (Fig 32). Their cells are described as **prokaryotic**; they are small, with very few structures (organelles) inside. In contrast, virtually all other organisms - plants, animals, fungi - are eukaryotic; they have large, relatively complex cells. About 1000 bacteria could fit into an average sized animal cell.

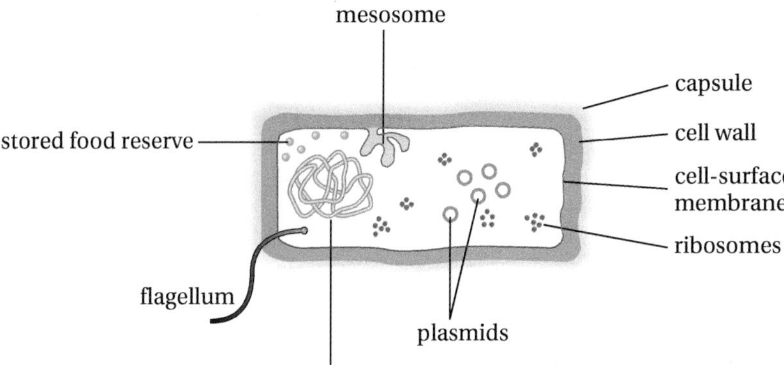

Fig 32
The basic structure of a bacterium. Notice that in prokaryotic cells there is no nuclear membrane

Viruses

Viruses are tiny infectious particles. They simply consist of some nuclear material surrounded by a protein coat, and an outer layer that allows them to gain entry to cells. The nuclear material is either DNA or RNA, and viral genomes consist of a relatively small number of genes.

Viruses are not normally classed as living because they do not have a cellular structure; they only perform one of the seven signs of life - reproduction - and they can't even do that on their own. Viruses must infect a living cell in order to reproduce.

Features of viral structure:

- Genetic material. All viruses contain DNA or RNA. Those containing RNA are called retroviruses and also contain the enzyme **reverse transcriptase**. This allows viruses to make DNA from RNA, which is transcription in reverse.
- **Capsid** - a protein layer that surrounds the genetic material.
- **Attachment proteins**. These are outside the capsid, and are used to attach to the host cell. The lock and key nature of this interaction explains why viruses are very specific to particular species, and often to particular cells (see HIV, page 44).

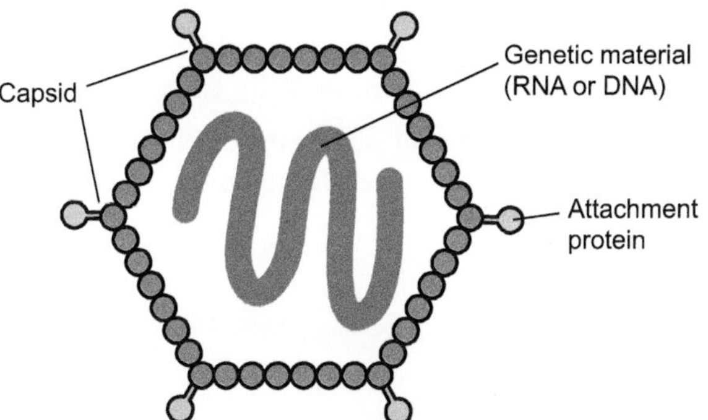

Fig 33 The structure of a virus particle

3.2.1.3 Methods of studying cells

Size and scaling

One millimetre is 1000 µm (**micrometres** or just microns) – cells and larger organelles that can generally be seen with a light microscope are measured in µm.

1 µm is 1000 nm (**nanometres**) – small organelles, such as ribosomes, and individual molecules are measured in nanometres. You need an electron microscope to see objects this small.

To work out the actual size of something in a photograph or diagram, you first measure it on the diagram and then use the **magnification** to work out its real size. For example, if the magnification was ×5000, each millimetre on the diagram would represent 1 five-thousandth of a millimetre in reality, which is 0.2 µm or 200 nm. If a mitochondrion measured 25 mm in the photograph, the actual size of the mitochondrion would be 0.2 × 25, which is 5 µm.

In microscopy questions, there are always three values:

- the actual size
- the size of the image, on paper or on the screen
- the magnification

which are connected by the formula:

$$\text{magnification} = \frac{\text{image size}}{\text{actual size}}$$

In exam questions you will be given two values – this often involves using a ruler – and you will have to work out the third. This may involve re-arranging the formula shown above.

You may find the following triangle useful:

I = Image size on paper
M = Magnification
A = Actual size

Scale bars

Sometimes you get a scale bar alongside the image, and this allows you to work out the magnification. If you get a scale bar like this:

|___0.5µm___|

you simply measure the length of the bar. For example, if the bar is 20 mm wide, and it says that it represents 0.5 µm, we know that the magnification is ×40 000 because 20 mm is 20 000 µm, and 20 000/0.5 = 40 000.

Cell fractionation

Individual organelles are easier to study when isolated from the rest of the cell. This can be done using **cell fractionation** and **ultracentrifugation**:

1 This breaks membranes and causes different parts of the cell and different substances to come into contact with each other. To minimise unusual reactions, a solution is added which:

Notes

The SI unit of length is the metre, m. In biology, we usually deal with much smaller units than this. You must be able to convert between numbers in standard and ordinary form.

1 mm = 10^{-3} m

1 µm = 10^{-6} m

1 nm = 10^{-9} m

Think, a nanometre is a thousandth of a thousandth of a thousandth of a metre. That's small.

Notes

It helps to practise conversion between units, and it basically involves working up and down in factors of 1000. For example, 0.35 µm can be converted into nanometers by multiplying up by 1000, making it 350 nm.

Notes

You must be able to work out the actual size of a cell or organelle when given the scale. Practise scaling calculations before examinations, and be familiar with the normal size of organelles so that you can recognise a silly answer when you see one.

- is ice cold to minimise enzyme activity
- is isotonic to prevent distortion of organelles due to water loss or gain ('osmotic damage')
- is a buffer, to prevent any pH changes.

2 The mixture is filtered to remove debris and then spun in an ultracentrifuge at high speed. The spinning greatly increases the gravitational field, and the organelles separate out according to density and, to some extent, shape.

3 First to separate out are the nuclei. The remaining fluid is poured off and **centrifuged** again to collect other organelles.

4 These are released in order of: mitochondria and lysosomes, rough ER, the plasma membranes and smooth ER and, finally, free ribosomes. With plant tissue, such as spinach leaf, the chloroplasts will separate out at around the same time as the mitochondria.

Essential Notes

Isotonic means 'of the same water potential' (see page 36). In this case, the fluid used has the same water potential as cell cytoplasm.

Different types of microscopy

There are two basic types of microscope:

- light, or optical
- electron.

Light microscopy uses light focused by lenses, whereas electron microscopy uses a beam of electrons, focused by magnets. Electron microscopes have a much greater **magnification** and, more importantly, a greater **resolution**, which is the ability to see detail. If a microscope has a maximum resolution of, say, 1 μm, then two objects closer together than 1 μm will appear to be one object.

The difference in resolution between the two types of microscope can be explained by the fact that the wavelength of light is much larger than the wavelength of a beam of electrons.

Scanning electron microscopes (SEMs) vs Transmission electron microscopes (TEMs)

The first electron microscopes, developed in the 1930s, were **transmission electron microscopes** (TEMs). They can only work on thin sections of material, so the images produced are two-dimensional, but they can have a very high resolution.

Scanning electron microscopes (SEMs) were developed later, and use computers to form an image as electrons bounce off the surface of the objects. The images produced are three-dimensional, but have a lower resolution than those produced by TEMs.

Notes

All of the images produced by both TEMs and SEMs are black and white, and the colour is added by computer afterwards, usually to make it easier to distinguish individual features.

3.2.2 All cells arise from other cells

All cells arise from other cells, by binary fission in prokaryotic cells and by **mitosis** and meiosis in eukaryotic cells.

Notes

The stages of mitosis – interphase, prophase, metaphase, anaphase and telophase – can be remembered with the mnemonic IPMAT.

Remembering that meta = middle and that ana = apart makes these stages easy to identify.

When interpreting diagrams or photographs, you can work out the stage of mitosis by the appearance of the chromosomes:

- two long strands = prophase
- two short strands and in the middle of the cell = metaphase
- short single strands near to the equator = anaphase
- single strands near to poles (or if the cell has started to divide) = telophase.

The cell cycle

The **cell cycle** is a series of events that start with the beginning of mitosis and ends when mitosis starts again in the daughter cell. The cycle therefore includes:

- The four phases of mitosis: **prophase**, **metaphase**, **anaphase** and **telophase**.
- The three phases of **interphase**, G1, S and G2.

The stages of mitosis are shown in Fig 34.

Mitosis

Mitosis is 'straightforward' cell division in which the DNA replicates and the cell splits to form two new cells. Each daughter cell receives an exact copy of the original DNA (unless there is a mutation). Organisms grow and repair themselves by mitosis.

Mitosis produces two daughter cells with identical genetic information: these cells are **clones** of the original cell. Before it divides by mitosis, a cell must first duplicate all of its DNA, and then organise the division so that each new cell gets a full set. DNA replication takes place *before* cell division, during interphase, while the DNA is spread out rather than condensed into chromosomes.

When DNA is spread out and diffuse in the nucleus, it is known as **chromatin**. Early in cell division the DNA condenses into chromosomes. The word chromosome means 'coloured body'. When chromosomes condense, they appear as double structures (Fig 35). This is a consequence of DNA replication. Each part of the chromosome – known as a **chromatid** – is identical. The two chromatids are held together by a **centromere**.

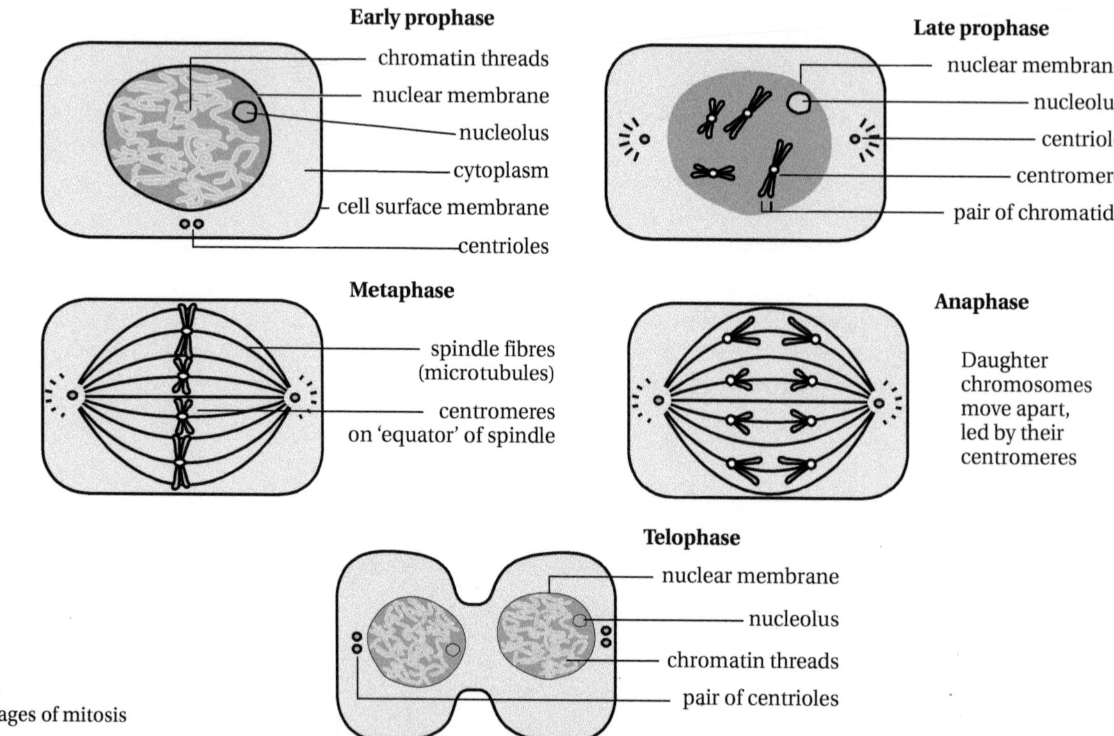

Fig 34
The stages of mitosis

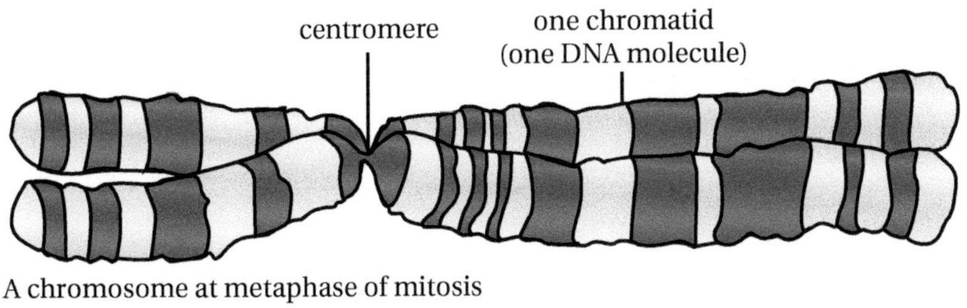

A chromosome at metaphase of mitosis

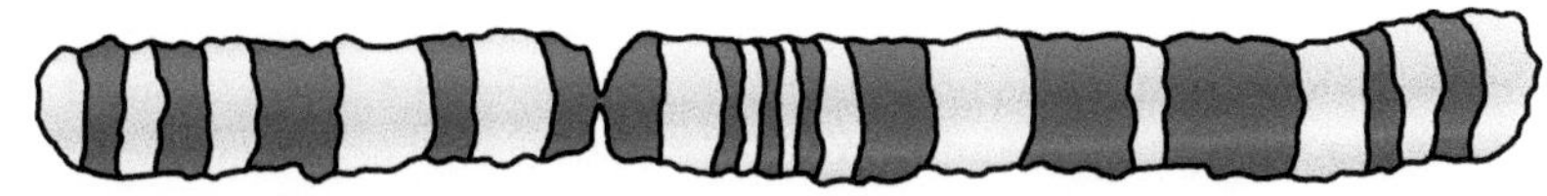
A chromosome at anaphase of mitosis, after the chromatids have separated

Fig 35
At the start of cell division, chromosomes appear as double structures consisting of two identical chromatids joined at the centromere. At anaphase, the paired chromosomes are pulled apart so each chromatid becomes a single chromosome. Note that the bands on the chromosomes in this diagram do *not* show individual genes

Division of the cytoplasm (**cytokinesis**) then usually occurs, producing two new cells. Interphase is the period of time between the start of one round of cell division and the start of the next. Most cells are in interphase most of the time. The chromosomes of cells in interphase are not visible because the DNA is spread out, and some of the genes are being **expressed** (translation is taking place and proteins are being produced).

Interphase has three distinct phases:

- **G1 (growth phase 1)** New organelles are made and the volume of cytoplasm increases. If the cell is not going to divide, it will stay in the G1 phase, carrying out its normal functions. Immediately after mitosis the daughter cells are small, with a relatively large nucleus. As the cell matures the volume of cytoplasm increases until the cell reaches full size. When the cell is ready to divide again, it goes into the next two phases of interphase.
- **S (synthesis phase)** DNA is replicated.
- **G2 (growth phase 2)** The cell makes specific enzymes and other proteins needed to complete mitosis.

The mitotic index

The **mitotic index** (MI) is a value that gives an indication of the turnover of a particular tissue or sample. The more rapidly the cells are dividing, the higher the index. The number of cells undergoing mitosis can be found using an optical microscope from the number of cells with visible chromosomes.

The mitotic index is calculated as follows:

$$\text{MI} = \frac{\text{cells with visible chromosomes}}{\text{total number of cells in sample}} \times 100$$

For example, if there are 50 cells in a field of view and 8 are in some stage of mitosis, the mitotic index is $\frac{8}{50} = 0.16$.

Cancer – mitosis out of control

Cells in the human body usually only divide when they should, in order to allow growth or the repair of tissues. At any one time, most cells are not dividing, they are in interphase. When the mechanisms that control the cell cycle break down, the result is the uncontrolled division, resulting in a swelling or growth known as a **tumour**.

Treatment of cancer

Broadly speaking, there are three treatments for cancer; surgery, chemotherapy and radiotherapy.

- **Surgery** involves cutting out the tumour - simple in principle, but some tumours can be very difficult to cut out. They may be located in a vital organ, or near vital blood vessels or nerves. It is also sometimes difficult to tell where the margins of the tumour are. This creates the double problem of needing to remove the entire tumour while preserving the healthy tissue.
- **Radiotherapy** involves treating the tumour with high doses of radiation, usually X-rays. High doses of radiation kill cells. The radiation can be focused on the tumour from an external source (an X-ray machine), or by placing radioactive material in or next to the tumour.
- **Chemotherapy** involves the injection of drugs that trael to all parts of the body. An ideal anti-cancer drug will target the tumour cells while leaving normal body cells unharmed, but this is not easy. Mitosis in the tumour is more rapid than in other tissues, and many anti-cancer drugs interfere with mitosis in some way. This also leads to damage in other areas of rapid mitosis such as bone marrow, skin and gut lining, but these normal cells usually recover once treatment is over.

Binary fission in prokaryotes

Prokaryotic cells (i.e. bacteria) reproduce by **binary fission**, which simply means 'splitting in half'. In ideal conditions, some bacteria can reproduce every ten minutes or so. When food is plentiful, bacteria can increase the cytoplasmic volume very quickly, and so they just need to copy their genetic material in order to divide. Binary fission is asexual and so is an example of cloning. However, bacteria are so numerous and reproduce so quickly that mutations are relatively common. This is an important source of new alleles which allow bacteria to evolve quickly, for example by developing antibiotic resistance.

Viral reproduction

Viruses do not undergo cell division, because they do not have a cellular structure. They can only reproduce inside living cells, which they do by taking over the cell's own ability to make new proteins and nucleic acids.

The viral life cycle is basically as follows:

1. The virus uses its attachment proteins (see page 31) to bind to a living cell. The attachment proteins must be complementary to those on the cell-surface membrane.
2. The virus gains entry to the cell, by a process similar to phagocytosis (see page 39), because the virus often becomes coated with the membrane of the cell.
3. The attachment proteins and the capsid dis-assemble, leaving free nucleic acid.
4. Sometimes, the viral DNA is actually incorporated into the chromosomes of the host cell.

5. The viral genes are expressed (transcribed and translated), and the proteins made are used to make more viral particles.
6. The new viral particles burst out of the cell, killing it in the process, and go on to infect new cells. The symptoms of viral disease are caused by the damage done to host cells, and by the toxins released as part of the process.

3.2.3 Transport across cell membranes

The structure of the cell membrane

This section is about cell membranes and how they work. First we look at the overall structure of the membrane. The basic structure of all cell membranes, including cell-surface membranes and the membranes around the cell organelles of eukaryotes, is the same.

The basic structure of the **plasma membrane**, or **cell surface membrane** (Fig 36) is described by the **fluid mosaic model**: 'mosaic' because there are many proteins in the membrane dotted around in a mosaic pattern, and 'fluid' because the pattern of proteins is continually changing. The membrane has very little physical strength at all, it's very thin (about 7–10 nm), but it does have a vital part to play in the control of what enters and leaves the cell.

Notes

The basic fluid mosaic structure is the same for all membranes, both in and around the cell. In Fig 28 every line is a membrane.

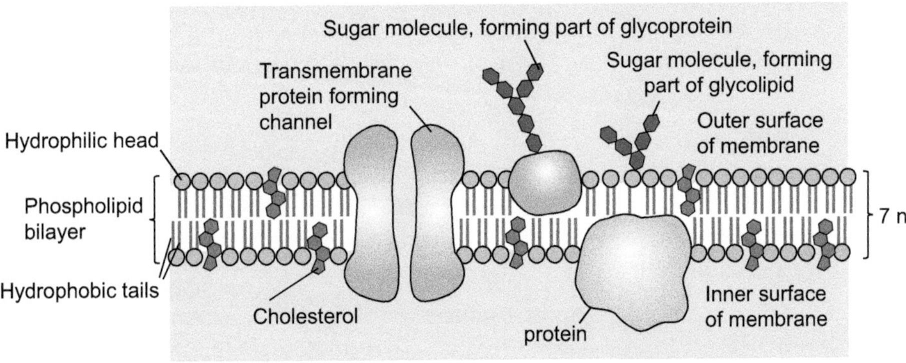

Fig 36
'Protein icebergs in a lipid sea' is one way to describe the fluid mosaic model of the plasma membrane.

The plasma membrane is made up of a phospholipid bilayer and proteins. The **phospholipid** bilayer forms a barrier to water-soluble substances such as sugars, amino acids and ions (for example, Na^+, Cl^-). Water itself can pass through the membrane with relative ease. Lipid-soluble substances, such as vitamins A, D, E and K, can pass freely across the membrane, as can the gases oxygen and carbon dioxide.

The proteins embedded in cell membranes have a variety of functions:

- They act as hydrophilic pores through which water-soluble chemicals can pass. However, large water-soluble compounds, such as large proteins, may be too big to pass through the pores and so may be unable to enter the cell at all.
- They are sites of **active transport** and **facilitated diffusion** (see below).
- They form *specific* **receptor sites** for hormones and other substances, which means that hormones can have an effect on some cells and not others.

- **Glycolipids** are phospholipids attached to short chains of sugar molecules, while **glycoproteins** are proteins attached to sugars. They have many different functions, mainly concerned with cell signalling and cell recognition, by the immune system, for example.
- **Cholesterol** molecules fit into between the phospholipids. They are much more common in animal cell membranes than in plant cells, where their function is to make the membrane more rigid and stable by reducing the sideways movement of the phospholipids. Red blood cells, for example, have more cholesterol than many other cells because they need to maintain their shape without support from surrounding cells and structures.

Movement in and out of cells

There are four basic processes by which individual molecules or ions can pass through membranes:

- diffusion
- facilitated diffusion
- osmosis
- active transport.

Larger volumes of liquid or solid can also pass into the cell by **endocytosis** or out of the cell by **exocytosis**.

Definition

Diffusion is the movement of particles from a region of relatively high concentration to a region of lower concentration until evenly spread.

Diffusion

Diffusion is a simple idea; particles spread out. Gases and liquids can diffuse, but solids cannot. If a substance is in higher concentration in one place compared to another, the particles will move around randomly until they become evenly spread. That's diffusion.

Diffusion is a **passive** process – substances will move down a concentration gradient without any input of energy in the form of ATP from the cell. The rate of diffusion depends on:

- the difference in concentration, i.e. the concentration gradient
- the distance over which diffusion occurs
- the surface area between the two regions
- the temperature. The higher the temperature, the more kinetic energy the particles possess, so they move around faster and diffuse faster.

Essential Notes

Remember, if you see the word *diffusion*, that net movement of molecules is always **down**, or *along* the concentration gradient, from high to low.

In order to increase the rate of diffusion, organisms must maximise surface area and concentration difference, and minimise the distance between the two areas. Organs that are adapted for exchange processes, such as the lungs and gills, illustrate this idea. They all have a large surface area, good blood supply (to maintain the concentration difference) and thin membranes.

Facilitated diffusion

Diffusion is said to be **facilitated diffusion** when it is speeded up by specific proteins in cell membranes. These proteins pass substances across the membrane faster than would otherwise be possible. This is *not* the same as active transport (below) because facilitated diffusion occurs *along a concentration gradient*, and *requires no metabolic energy*.

There are two types of protein responsible for facilitated diffusion:

1. **Carrier proteins.** These proteins bind to the substance to be transported and then change their shape - biochemists call it a *conformational* change - so that the substance is transported to the other side of the membrane. Often, carrier proteins operate by co transport - two substances are transported together, such as sodium and glucose, or sodium and an amino acid. Carrier proteins are also responsible for active transport.
2. **Channel proteins.** These are more like pores (think 'holes'). The proteins form gaps through which particular water soluble particles, such as chloride ions, can pass. These are different from carrier proteins because they do not bind tightly to the molecules they transport, nor do they change their shape in order to move them. They can, however, change their shape to open or close.

Osmosis

Osmosis is the diffusion of water. When two solutions are separated by a **partially permeable membrane**, which prevents at least some of the solutes moving across, water molecules will move, along *their* concentration gradient. In other words, if the solute can't diffuse to the water, the water will diffuse to the solute.

A more correct way of defining osmosis is in terms of water potential. **Water potential** is a measure of how easy it is for water to move: water in a dilute solution can move more freely than water in a concentrated solution. Water potentials are measured in pressure units, usually kPa. *Pure water* is given a water potential of 0 kPa.

Water in any solution can move less freely than in pure water, so *all* solutions have a *negative* water potential. A dilute solution will have a less negative water potential (for example, –100 kPa) than a more concentrated solution (for example, –300 kPa). If these solutions were separated by a differentially

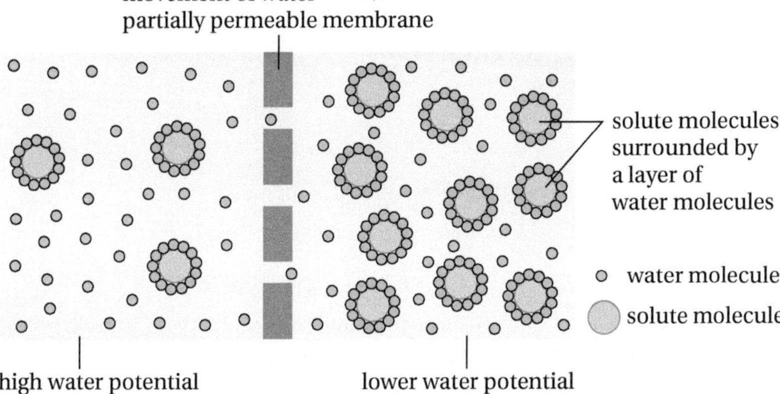

Fig 37
Osmosis occurs when two solutions of different concentration are separated by a partially permeable membrane

Notes
Note the expression 'partially permeable' is preferred by examiners to the terms 'differentially permeable' and 'selectively permeable'.

Notes
Facilitated diffusion can be done by either carrier proteins or channel proteins. Active transport can only be done by carrier proteins.

Notes
Many candidates have an instinctive understanding of osmosis, but fail to gain full marks because of incorrect use of terminology. Instead of talking about 'strong' and 'weak' solutions, make sure you can describe situations in terms of water potential.

Definition
Water potential is a measure of the tendency of a solution cell to absorb water by osmosis or for water to move out of a solution.

Notes
Osmosis happens because molecules in solution attract a shell of water molecules which are therefore not free to move around. Osmosis can be explained in three words: *solute attracts solvent*.

permeable membrane, water would pass from the less negative value (the dilute solution where the water can move more freely) to the more negative value (the more concentrated solution where water can move less freely). This is shown in Fig 37. The most negative water potential you are ever likely to come across is that of *dry air*. This is why water evaporates and is a vital force in the water cycle on this planet.

So the more accurate definition of osmosis is:

Definition

Osmosis is the movement of water from a region of less negative water potential to a region of more negative water potential across a partially permeable membrane.

Notes

Investigating the water potential of plant tissue (usually referred to as 'osmosis in spuds') involves finding the concentration of an unknown solution by producing a **dilution series** of a solute to produce a **calibration curve**.

Investigating the **permeability** of cell-surface membranes could involve comparing the amount of pigment that leaks from beetroot as the cell-surface membranes are damaged by temperature or alcohol.

In both cases a **colorimeter** could be used to measure the absorbance (depth of colour) of a solution.

Osmosis in animal cells

Three terms are commonly used when discussing osmosis in animal cells:

- **Hypertonic** describes a solution that has a *more negative* water potential than another (it is more concentrated). For example, sea water is hypertonic to blood.
- **Isotonic** describes a solution that has the *same* water potential/concentration as another. For example, Ringer's solution can be used to keep tissues alive because it is isotonic to blood plasma.
- **Hypotonic** describes a solution that has a *less negative* water potential than another (it is less concentrated). For example, pure water is hypotonic to blood so, when we drink it, water is absorbed into our blood.

Animal cells are not surrounded by a strong cell wall. So, when they are placed in a solution of higher water potential, such as pure water, they swell up and burst. For this reason animals need to **osmoregulate** – they need to control the concentration of their body fluids. In vertebrates the main organ of osmoregulation is the kidney.

One of the most remarkable feats of the mammalian kidney is its ability to produce urine that is hypertonic to blood. So, when water is in short supply, we can still get rid of waste without losing too much precious water.

Active transport

Diffusion, facilitated diffusion and osmosis are passive; they involve the movement of substances down a diffusion gradient and therefore do not require an input of energy. Active transport is a mechanism that allows organisms to move substances across membranes *against* a diffusion gradient, for example, to allow organisms to absorb a rare trace element, or to remove virtually all of a toxic waste. Active transport makes exchange processes *more efficient*.

Essential features of active transport mechanisms are:

- Substances move *against* a concentration gradient, i.e. from low to high.
- The process requires energy in the form of ATP.
- There are specific carrier proteins in the cell membrane.
- If respiration is inhibited, for example, by a lack of oxygen, active transport slows down or stops.

Cells adapted for active transport, such as those lining the intestine (page 23) or kidney tubule, show two key adaptations:

- **Microvilli** greatly increase the membrane surface area, which means there can be more carrier proteins/pumps.
- The presence of numerous mitochondria to provide the ATP required.

Co-transport

Both glucose and amino acids pass into the blood by a mechanism called co-transport, in which they are both absorbed along with sodium ions, via a specific membrane protein. This is covered more fully in AQA Biology AS/A-level Year 1 Topics 3 and 4.

3.2.4 Cell recognition and the immune system

An **antigen** is a molecule – usually a protein or carbohydrate – on the surface of a cell, which identifies the type of cell.

Cell-surface antigens enable the **immune system** to identify:

- **pathogens** (such as bacteria or viruses)
- cells from other organisms of the same species (such as from an organ transplant)
- abnormal body cells (in which the DNA has been altered, such as in a tumour)
- toxins (such as those secreted by pathogens).

When any of these cells enter the body, the outer surface is recognised as 'foreign' or 'non-self' because it is made up of many antigens that are not normally found in the host's body. **Active immunity** involves recognising the pathogen or antigen that has entered the body, and making complementary **antibodies** to prevent it multiplying.

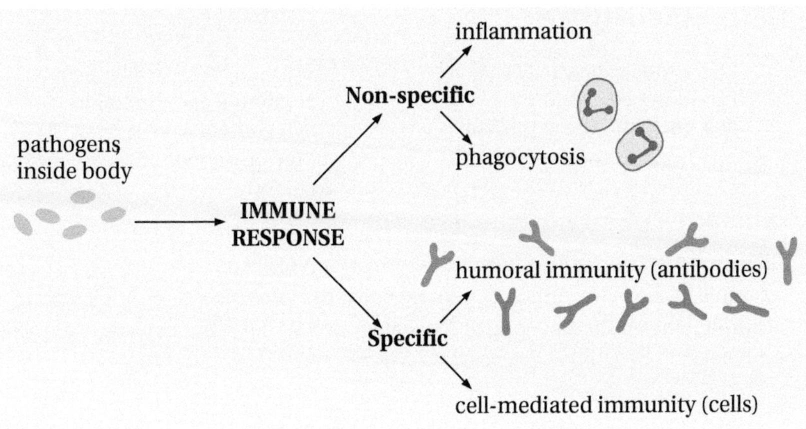

Fig 38
An overview of the body's imumne responses: non-specific responses are general responses to damage. They include **inflammation** and **phagocytosis** of debris. Specific responses are targeted against individual types of microorganism.

Phagocytosis

In this process, the most common type of white cells, the **neutrophils**, engulf any foreign material that has entered the body, such as small particles of dust in the lungs, or bacteria at the site of infection. Fig 39 shows the essential stages of **phagocytosis**.

Essential Notes

White blood cells are sometimes just called white cells because many of them spend most of their time out of the blood.

Fig 39
Phagocytosis

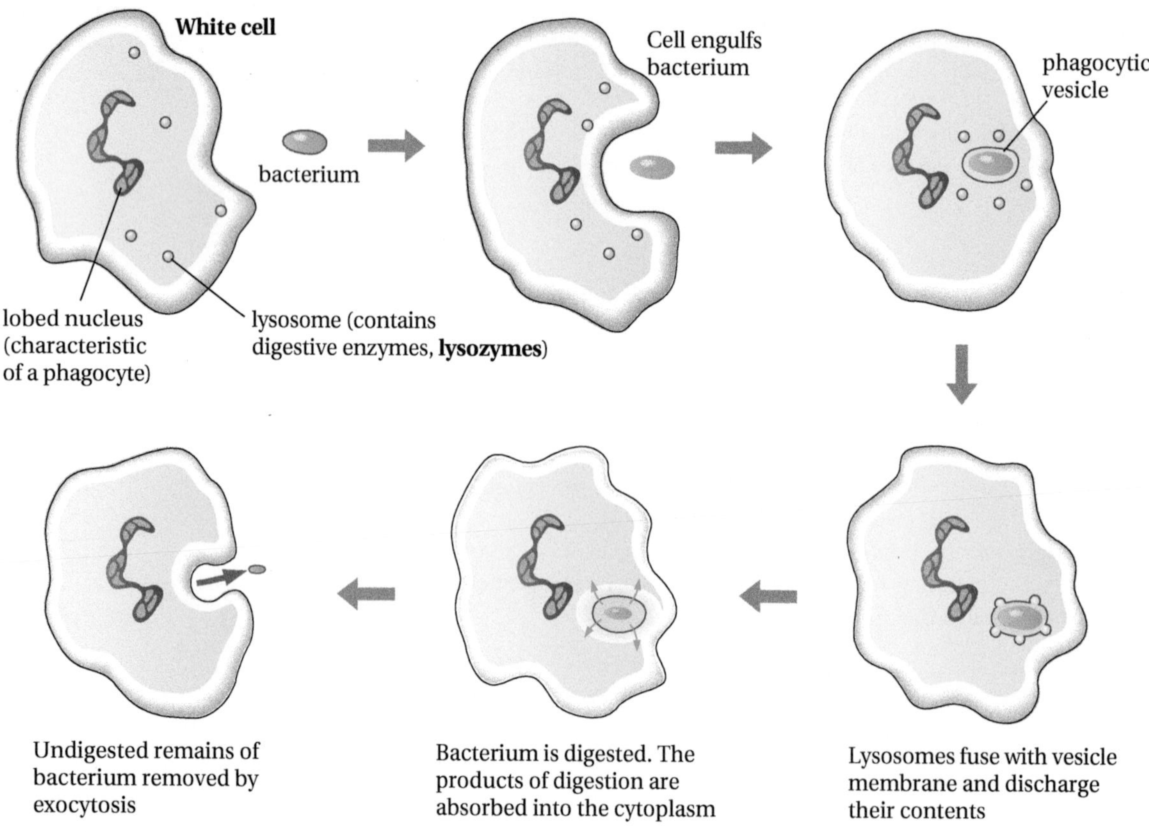

Notes

In examination answers about the immune system there is too much talk of 'fighting'. Try to avoid this description.

The specific immune system

This aspect of immunity involves the recognition of specific pathogens. For example, if the polio virus gets into the body, the immune system will respond by producing antibodies specific for that virus, and not other viruses.

When a particular pathogen gets into the body, the immune system is activated as follows:

1. The pathogen is recognised as non-self by the antigens on its surface, and engulfed by a **phagocyte** (a type of white blood cell).
2. The phagocyte takes the antigens from the pathogen and 'displays' them on its outer membrane. In doing so it becomes an **antigen-presenting cell**.
3. The presented antigens are detected by **helper T cells** (also called T_H cells), which become activated.
4. In turn, the T_H cells stimulate three other types of cell:
   - **cytotoxic T cells** (T_C cells, or killer T cells), a type of **T lymphocyte**
   - **B lymphocytes (B cells)**
   - **phagocytes.**
5. The B cells then multiply into **plasma cells** and **memory cells.** Plasma cells release large amounts of antibodies into the blood but are short lived. Memory cells, on the other hand, are long lived and can survive in the body for years.

There are two different aspects to the specific immune response: the **cellular response** (Fig 41), which is carried out by the cells, and the **humoral response** (Fig 42), which is carried out by **antibodies.** A 'humour' is a fluid, so humoral immunity refers to the fact that the antibodies are in the plasma and tissue fluid.

The cellular and humoral immune responses

The cellular response is carried out by the **cytotoxic T (T_C) cells**, where the cell itself attacks the pathogen. T_C cells attach to the pathogen and either inject toxins into it, causing its death, or label the pathogen for phagocytosis (see above).

The humoral response involves B cells which, when exposed to an antigen, form **plasma cells.** These cells produce and secrete antibodies to a specific antigen. A small number remain as **memory cells.** If cells carrying the same antigen enter the blood again, the memory cells 'recognise' them and produce new plasma cells faster than before. We are immune to a particular disease as long as we have memory cells.

Notes

There are many different types of white cells but the three basic types you need to know about are:

- B lymphocytes (B cells)
- T lymphocytes (T cells)
- Phagocytes.

Both B and T cells make antibodies. Phagocytes, sometimes called macrophoges, carry out phagocytosis.

Fig 40
The cellular response to an antigen

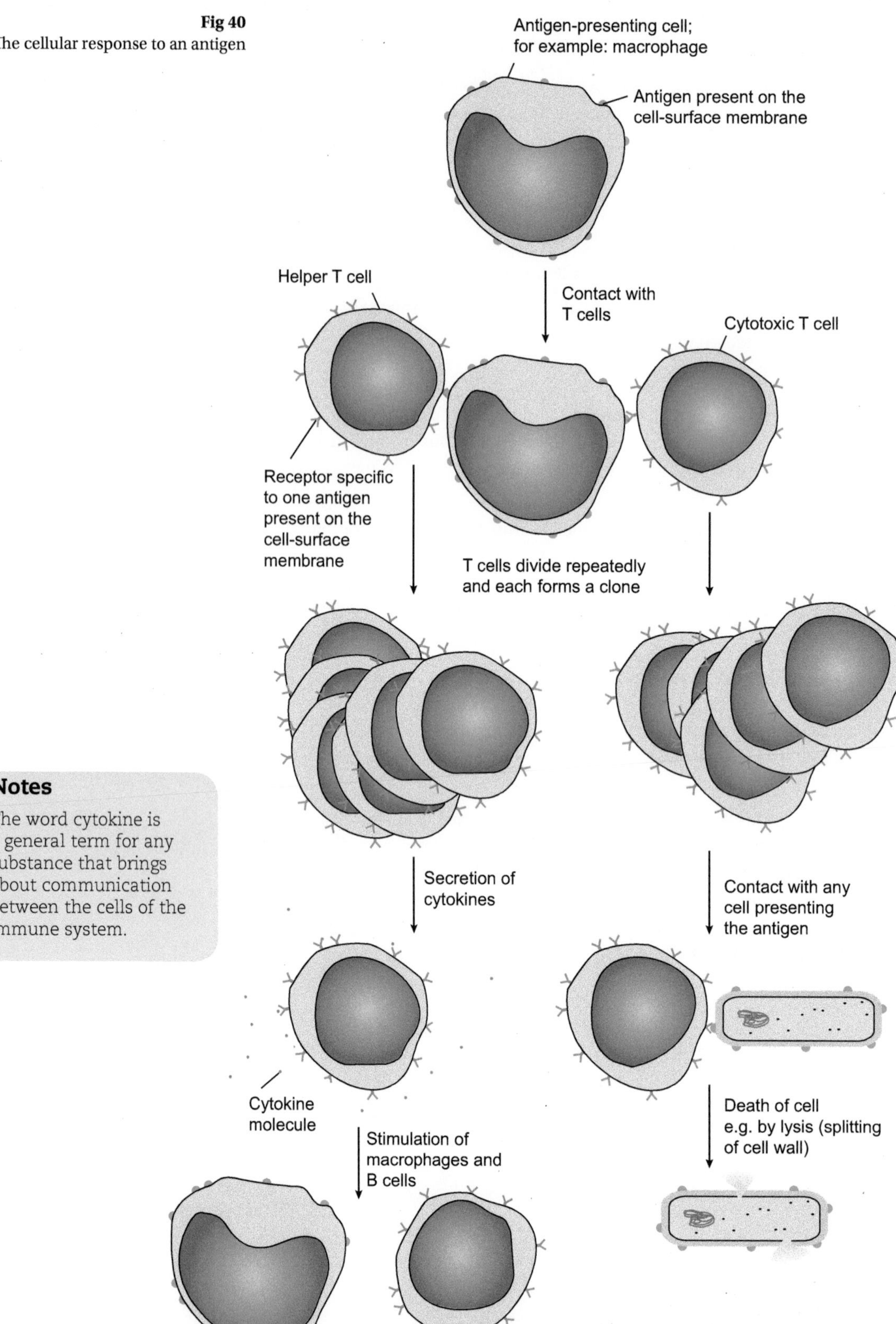

Notes

The word cytokine is a general term for any substance that brings about communication between the cells of the immune system.

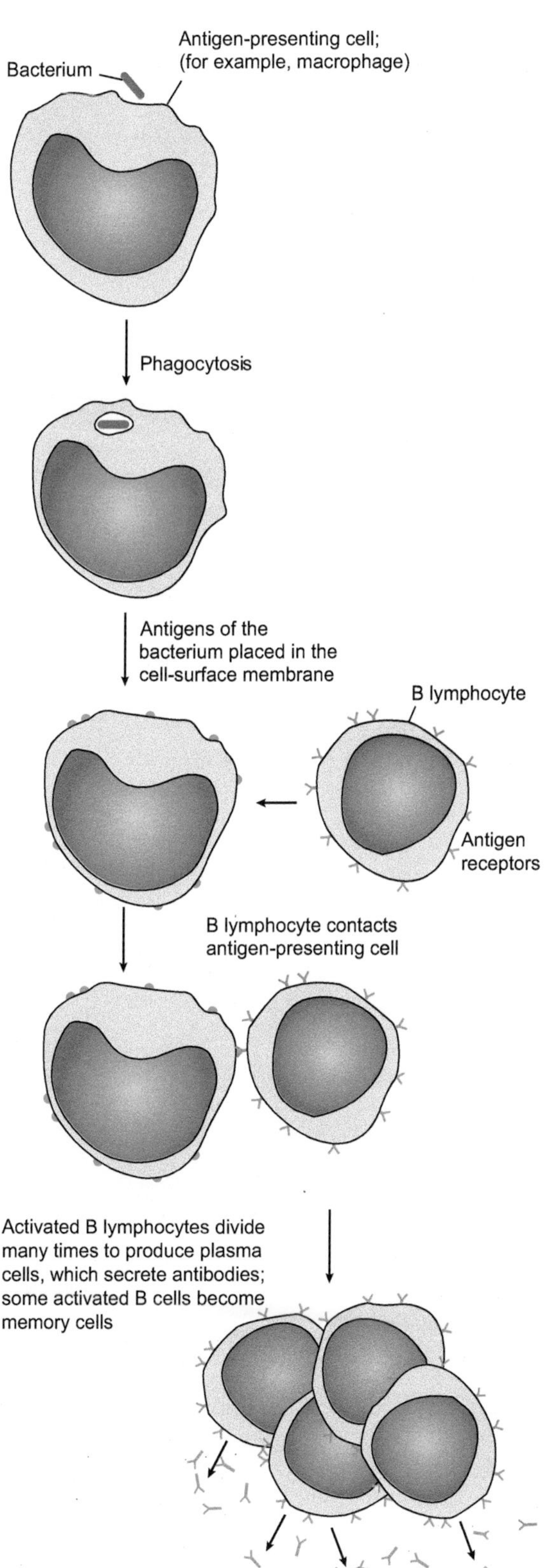

Fig 41
The humoral response to an antigen

The immune system develops by clonal selection

If the body is to survive exposure to a particular pathogen, it needs to be able to make antibodies in relatively large quantities. The problem is; we can only make enough antibodies to a particular disease if we have already been exposed to the pathogen. How do we survive that first exposure?

Before birth, a baby grows and develops in a sterile environment, and gets antibodies via the placenta so that when it is born it already has some immunity. After birth, the baby continues to get antibodies from its mother via her milk. This is **passive immunity**. When the body is stimulated to makes its own antibodies, this as **active immunity**.

After birth, a baby is exposed to a variety of pathogens. The immune system develops by a process called **clonal selection**. At birth, we have millions of different small populations of genetically identical of B cells – 'clones' – each capable of making a particular antibody. The T cells activate the B cells capable of making the right antibody – they 'select a clone'. The B cells multiply into a large population of plasma cells and memory cells.

Notes

Antibiotics are no use for fighting viral infections. Antibiotics are effective against bacteria because they interfere with some aspect of prokaryote metabolism, leaving eukaryotic cells unharmed. Viruses have very little metabolism to speak of.

The primary and secondary immune response

The production of plasma and memory cells can take weeks and is known as the **primary immune response**.

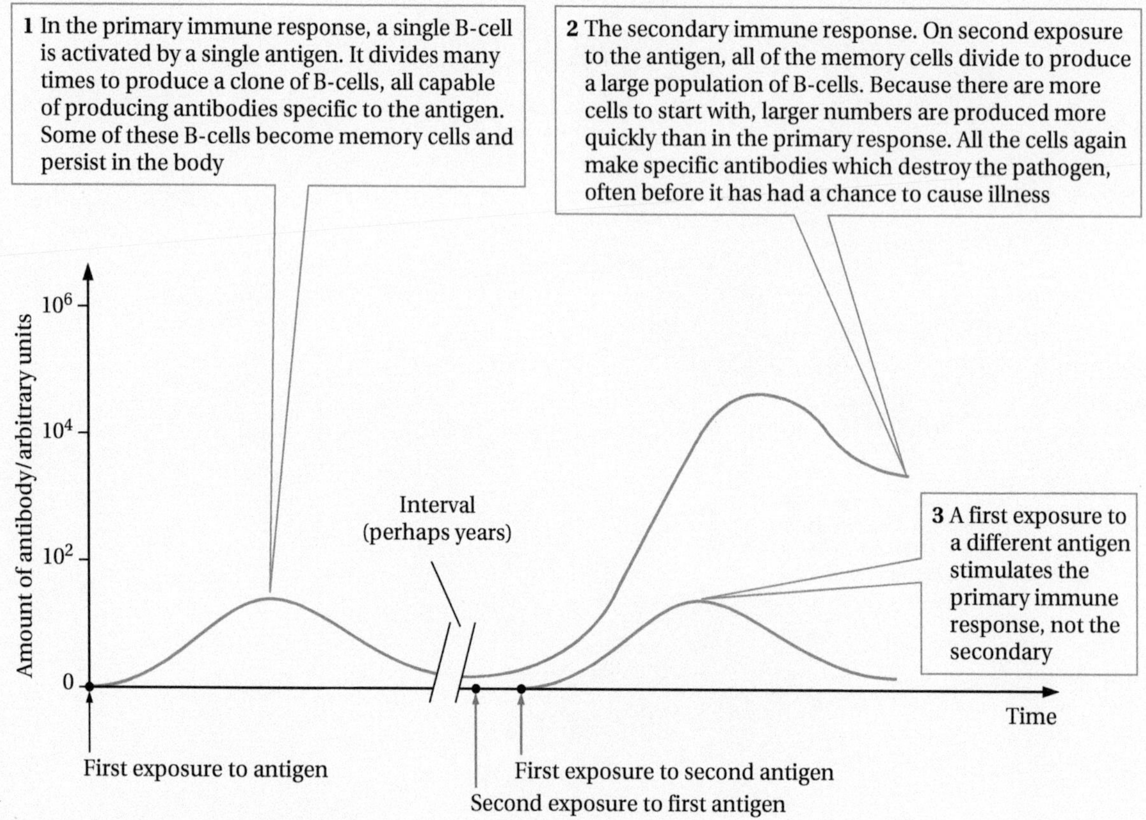

Fig 42
The primary and secondary immune responses

When the pathogen or antigen gets into the body for the second time, the memory cells quickly multiply into a large population of plasma calls that can produce the required antibody quickly to fight the infection. This is the **secondary immune response**. The secondary response is faster, many times greater and more prolonged than the primary response (Figure 42). The antibodies made by a particular clone are all identical and are known as **monoclonal antibodies.**

The use of monoclonal antibodies (MABs)

MABs are antibodies that are made by one specific clone of B cells, so they are all identical. MABs are very specific, and have many uses in medicine because they can detect minute quantities of a particular substance in the body.

A classic example of the use MABs is in pregnancy tests, where they are used to detect the hormone HCG, produced in minute amounts by the developing foetus. The antibodies attach to the hormone, and the hormone-antibody complex fixes an enzyme in place. The enzyme makes a coloured product, which creates a visible result, such as a blue line.

MABs can also be used to deliver drugs to specific targets, for example anti-cancer agents can be delivered right to specific tumour cells. The tumour cells will have specific proteins on their cell-surface membrane, to which the MABs will bind.

HIV and AIDS

HIV stands for Human Immunodeficiency Virus. It is a retrovirus, so it contains RNA and the enzyme reverse transcriptase. Once inside the body, the virus is very specific, and only infects a particular type of lymphocyte known as a T4 helper cell. The viral RNA is turned into DNA using the enzyme, which becomes incorporated into the chromosomes of the T helper cells, and is copied each time these cells divide.

There is usually a latent period when there are no symptoms, often lasting years, before the viral DNA becomes activated. When it does, the DNA is transcribed and translated, using the host cell's ribosomes and other organelles to make more viral particles. The new particles break out of the host cells and infect more T helper cells. In this way, the number of functional T helper cells decreases, until a threshold is reached when active immunity is no longer effective and the body falls victim to infections that it would normally fight off.

The ELISA test

ELISA stands for **enzyme-linked immunosorbant assay.** These are very sensitive tests that can detect minute quantities of substances, such as antigens, in the body. They usually use a combination of monoclonal antibodies, antigens and enzymes. The HIV test is a good example of an ELISA test. An individual who has been infected with HIV has tiny amounts of viral antibodies in their plasma, but the ELISA test is sensitive enough to detect their presence. Fig 43 shows the general idea behind an ELISA test.

Viral antigens are attached to a solid surface

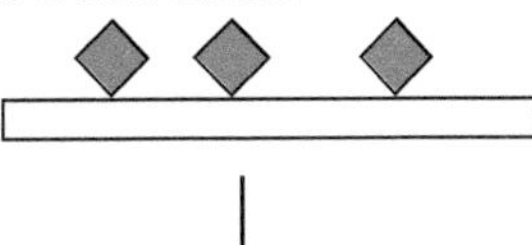

Antibody for the virus is attached to an enzyme and the antibody binds to the virus

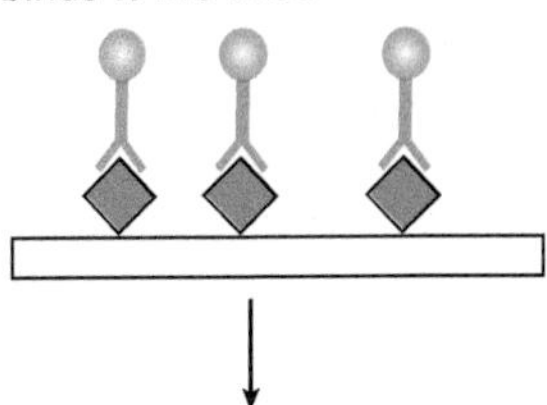

The substrate for the enzyme is added and is changed to a product that has a different colour

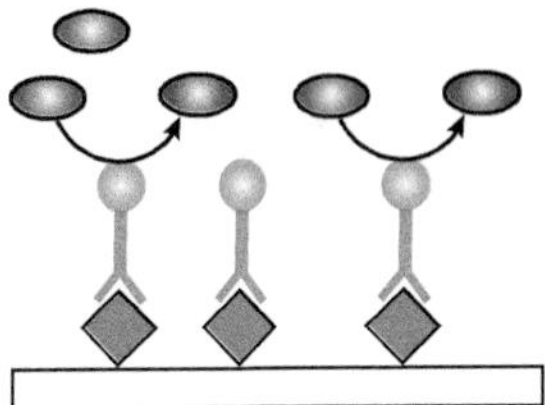

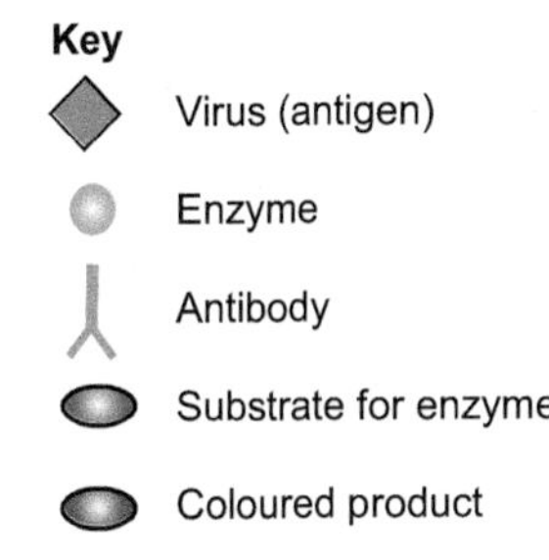

Fig 43
The ELISA test

Vaccinations

Humans have survived for thousands or years without effective medical help. However, until the 20th century, infant mortality was very high throughout the world. A large proportion of children - up to 50% or more - did not survive until their fifth birthday because of a combination of infectious disease and malnutrition. A major step towards reducing infant mortality in developed countries was the development of vaccines.

Vaccines usually contain either the pathogen or the antigens, treated so that they cannot cause the disease. The idea is to stimulate the primary response, so that when the actual pathogen is encountered, the secondary response is strong enough to prevent the disease developing.

There are several different types of vaccine:

- **Live, attenuated vaccines** - these contain pathogens that have been treated in some way so that they can divide a few times in the body but cannot set up an infection. Measles, mumps and rubella can all be prevented by live vaccines.
- **Dead microorganisms** - these obviously cannot cause the disease but they contain the antigens that stimulate the immune response, e.g. diphtheria.
- **Purified antigens** - often made by genetic engineering, for example, hepatitis B.

Essential Notes

A **vaccine** is the actual fluid that is injected or swallowed. **Vaccination** is the process of administering the vaccine. The terms **vaccination** and **immunisation** basically refer to the same process.

The problems with flu vaccines

The influenza virus shows **antigenic variation**. It is able to change the proteins on its outer coat. Each new strain of virus that emerges has different antigens, and so any antibodies made in response to previous strains are no use. This is why vulnerable people such as the elderly are offered flu vaccines every winter.

Practical and mathematical skills

In both the AS and A level papers at least 15% of marks will be allocated to the assessment of skills related to practical work. A minimum of 10% of the marks will be allocated to assessing mathematical skills at level 2 and above. These practical and mathematical skills are likely to overlap to some extent, for example, applying mathematical concepts to analysing given data and in plotting and interpretation of graphs.

The required practical activities assessed at AS are:

- Investigation into the effect of a named variable on the rate of an enzyme-controlled reaction.
- Preparation of stained squashes of cells from plant root tips; setup and use of an optical microscope to identify the stages of mitosis in these stained squashes and calculation of a mitotic index.
- Production of a dilution series of a solute to produce a calibration curve with which to identify the water potential of plant tissue.
- Investigation into the effect of a named variable on the permeability of cell-surface membranes.
- Dissection of animal or plant gas exchange system or mass transport system or of organ within such a system.
- Use of aseptic techniques to investigate the effect of antimicrobial substances on microbial growth.

The additional required practical activities assessed only at A level are:

- Use of chromatography to investigate the pigments isolated from leaves of different plants, e.g. leaves from shade-tolerant and shade-intolerant plants or leaves of different colours.
- Investigation into the effect of a named factor on the rate of dehydrogenase activity in extracts of chloroplasts.
- Investigation into the effect of a named variable on the rate of respiration of cultures of single-celled organisms.
- Investigation into the effect of an environmental variable on the movement of an animal using either a choice chamber or a maze.
- Production of a dilution series of a glucose solution and use of colorimetric techniques to produce a calibration curve with which to identify the concentration of glucose in an unknown 'urine' sample.
- Investigation into the effect of a named environmental factor on the distribution of a given species.

Questions will assess the ability to understand in detail how to ensure that the use of instruments, equipment and techniques leads to results that are as accurate as possible. The list of apparatus and techniques is given in the specification.

Exam questions may require problem solving and application of scientific knowledge in practical contexts, including novel contexts.

Exam questions may also ask for critical comments on a given experimental method, conclusions from given observations or require the presentation of data in appropriate ways, such as in tables or graphs. It will also be necessary to express numerical results to an appropriate precision with reference to uncertainties and errors, for example, in thermometer readings.

The mathematical skills assessed are given in the specification.

Practice exam-style questions

1 **Fig E1**

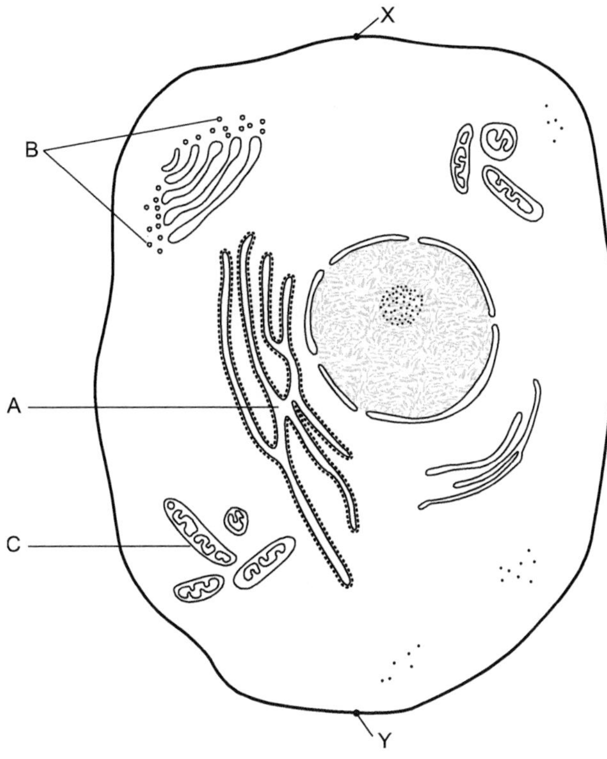

Above is a diagram of an animal cell, taken from a micrograph.

(a) Was the original micrograph taken using an electron or an optical (light) microscope? Explain your choice.

2 marks

(b) Name organelles A and B.

2 marks

(c) The diameter of the cell from X to Y is 20 μm. Calculate the magnification of the diagram.

2 marks

(d) The organelles that cover organelle A are 0.025 μm in diameter. Express this in nanometers.

1 mark

(e) The nucleus is roughly spherical and has a diameter of 8 μm. Calculate its volume in μm^3 from the formula:

volume $= \frac{4}{3}\pi r^3$

2 marks

(f) What is the function of the organelles labelled C?

1 mark

(g) The organelles labelled C in this cell are all the same shape. Suggest a reason for the fact that they appear to be different shapes.

1 mark

Total marks: 11

2 The complete life of a cell, the time between one cell division and the next, is known as the cell cycle.

(a) In what phase of the cell cycle does DNA replication occur?

1 mark

(b) Explain why it is essential that DNA replication occurs before mitosis.

2 marks

In a famous series of experiments in the 1950s, Meselsohn and Stahl showed that DNA replication was semi-conservative. Their basic experiment is outlined below:

Fig E2

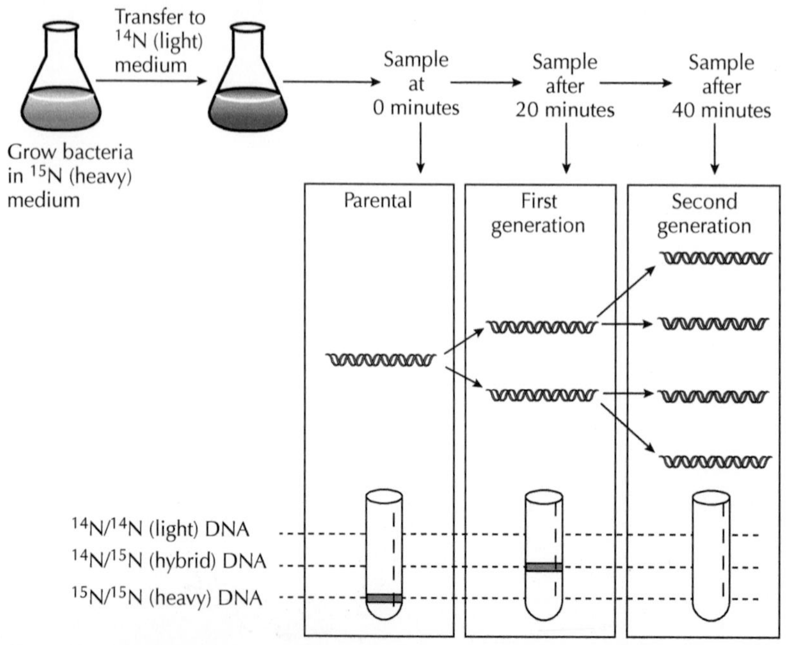

(c) Explain what is meant by semi-conservative replication.

____ 1 mark

(d) Outline the principles behind centrifugation.

____

____ 2 marks

(e) Explain why DNA containing hybrid $^{15}N/^{14}N$ formed a band above that of $^{15}N/^{15}N$.

____ 1 mark

(f) Complete the diagrams to show the positions of the bands in the second generation. Explain your answer.

____

____

____ 2 marks

Total marks: 9

3 The diagram shows the primary sequence of the protein lysozyme – an enzyme found in tears and sweat.

Fig E3

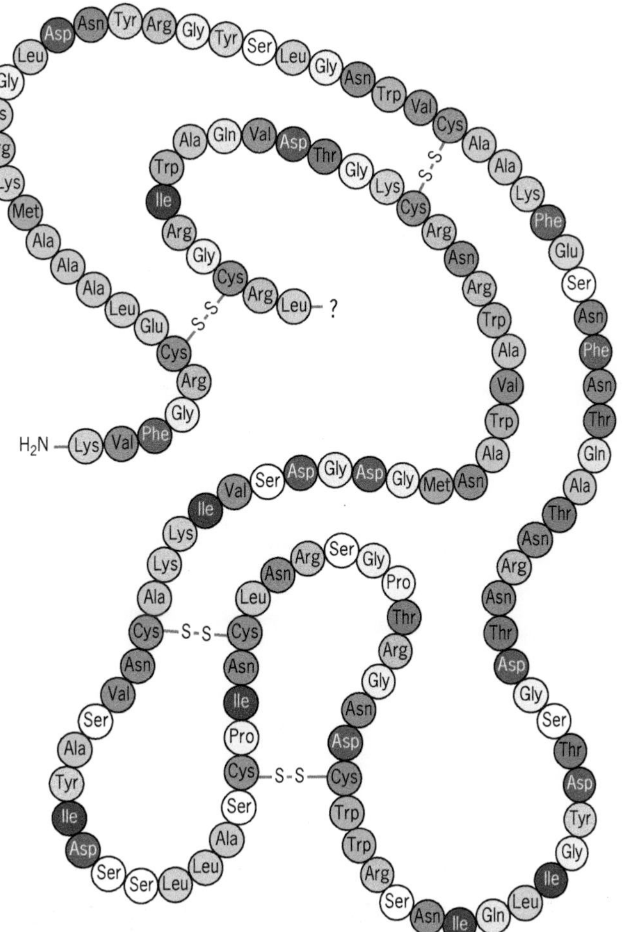

(a) The polypeptide chain of lysozyme has an $-NH_2$ group on one end – what chemical grouping should be at the other end?

1 mark

Trypsin is a protein-digesting enzyme that hydrolyses proteins by making a cut in the polypeptide chain wherever an argenine (Arg) is found next to a lysine (Lys).

(b) Into how many fragments would trypsin digest lysozyme?

1 mark

Enzymes are described as being specific.

(c) (i) What is meant by specificity?

1 mark

(ii) If enzymes are specific, explain how trypsin is able to digest a wide variety of different proteins, for example in pork, beef, chicken, milk and soya.

2 marks

Total marks: 5

4 A student carried out an investigation into the effect of pH on the activity of amylase, a starch-digesting enzyme.

The student set up seven test tubes containing starch solution and then added buffer solutions set at pH 3, 5, 7, 9 and 11. After they were thoroughly mixed, the amylase was added. At regular intervals, the student removed a drop of solution from each tube and tested for the presence of starch.

In the investigation:

(a) What was the independent variable?

1 mark

(b) What was the dependent variable?

1 mark

(c) State three variables that would need to be controlled.

3 marks

(d) Describe how the student could test for the presence of starch.

2 marks

(e) The teacher suggested that the buffer solutions could be digesting the starch. What control experiments should be carried out to validate the results of this experiment?

2 marks

(f) The graph shows the progress of an enzyme-controlled reaction.

Fig E4

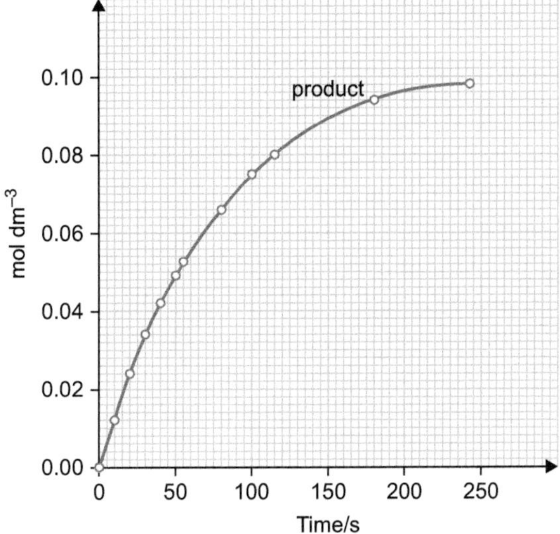

Use the graph to explain the term *rate of reaction.*

1 mark

(g) Use a tangent to work out the rate of reaction at 150 seconds.

2 marks

(h) On the graph, sketch the line that would be obtained if the *y* axis represented substrate (or reactant) concentration. 1 mark

Total marks: 13

5 The diagram shows the changes in the DNA content of a cell during cell division.

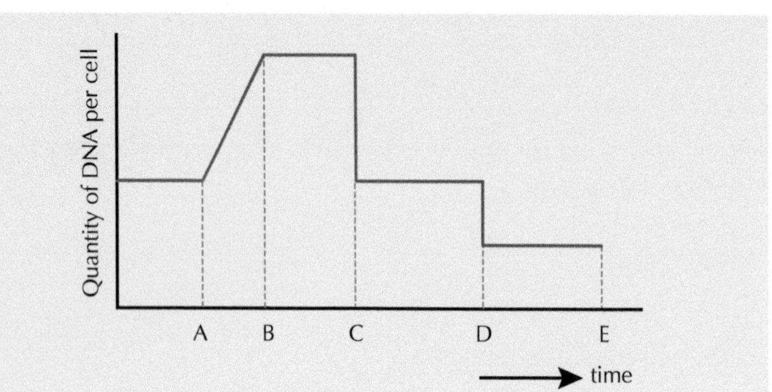

Fig E5

(a) Identify the type of cell division shown in the diagram. Give a reason for your answer.

____

____ 2 marks

(b) What is happening in the nucleus between A and B?

____ 1 mark

(c) What is happening to the cell at point C?

____ 1 mark

(d) Describe the appearance of the chromosomes between points C and D.

____

____

____ 2 marks

Total marks: 6

6 A student looked at a root tip preparation through a light microscope, and counted the number of cells in each phase of mitosis. The results are shown in the table.

Phase	Number of cells
Interphase	18
Prophase	20
Metaphase	14
Anaphase	4
Telophase	9

(a) How can you tell that this is a rapidly dividing tissue?

____ 1 mark

(b) Describe what happens to the chromosomes in anaphase.

____

____ 2 marks

(c) Suggest why there are so few cells in anaphase.

____ 1 mark

In a healthy individual, cell division is carefully controlled and cells only divide when they should. At any one time, the vast majority of somatic (body) cells are in interphase.

(d) Describe the appearance of the nucleus of a cell in interphase.

____ 2 marks

(e) How many chromosomes are present in a human somatic cell?

____ 1 mark

(f) Explain how mutations in a somatic cell can lead to the development of a tumour.

____

____ 3 marks

Total marks:10

7 The diagram illustrates the hydrolysis of a triglyceride.

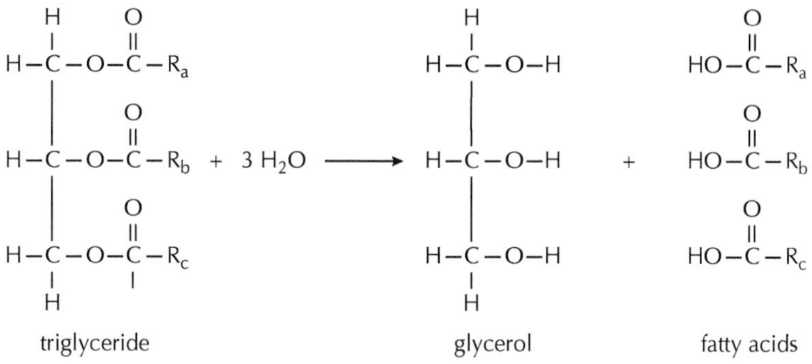

```
    H     O                              H                     O
    |     ||                             |                     ||
  H-C-O-C-Ra                           H-C-O-H              HO-C-Ra
    |                                    |
    |     O                              |                     O
    |     ||                             |                     ||
  H-C-O-C-Rb  +  3 H2O  ------>        H-C-O-H      +       HO-C-Rb
    |                                    |
    |     O                              |                     O
    |     ||                             |                     ||
  H-C-O-C-Rc                           H-C-O-H              HO-C-Rc
    |     |                              |
    H                                    H

   triglyceride                        glycerol            fatty acids
```

(a) Name the enzyme that would bring about this reaction

____ 1 mark

(b) What is represented by the three R groups, a b and c?

____

____ 1 mark

(c) Give two ways in which these R groups can vary

2 marks

A student investigated the digestion of the triglycerides in milk. She added enzyme to a and followed the progress of the reaction with a pH probe (a data logger).

This is the graph she obtained.

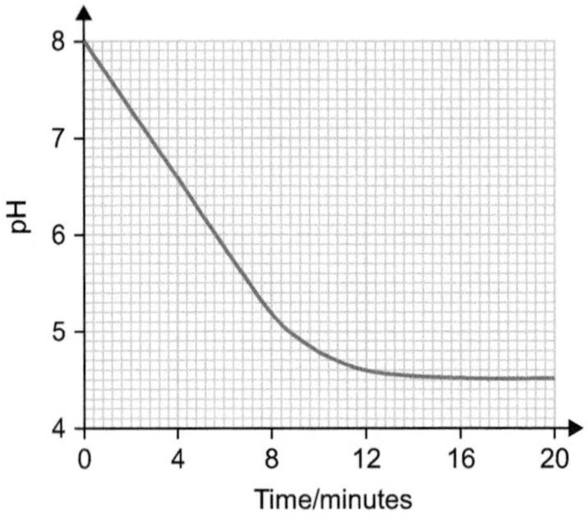

pH
Time/minutes

Fig E6

(d) Explain why the pH falls

1 mark

(e) Explain why the graph levels off

1 mark

(f) The rate of the reaction slows down.

Using tangents if necessary, work out the rates of reaction at 4 minutes and 10 minutes.

Use these values to calculate the ratio of the rates of reaction at 4 and 12 minutes.

Show your working.

3 marks

Total marks:9

8 The immune system is the body system that provides defence against disease.

(a) What is meant by the term antigen?

1 mark

(b) Explain how a vaccine gives an individual long-term resistance against a particular disease.

4 marks

(c) Explain why it is particularly difficult to develop an effective vaccine against influenza.

2 marks

(d) Suggest why some people may object to their child being given a particular vaccination.

1 mark

(e) In some circumstances, people with an infection may be treated by injecting antibodies directly into the bloodstream. Explain why this might be necessary.

2 marks

Total marks:10

9 Complete the table with ticks if the statement is true, crosses if not.

	Diffusion	Osmosis	Facilitated diffusion	Active transport
Takes place against a diffusion gradient				
Requires metabolic energy from the cell				
Requires a partially permeable membrane				
Requires specific proteins in the membrane				

Total marks:4

Answers

Question	Answer	Marks
1 (a)	Electron microscope Reason: resolution too high for a light microscope; any suitable example: can see ribosomes, can see cristae in mitochondria	2, 1 for answer, 1 for reason
1 (b)	A = Rough ER/Endoplasmic reticulum B = Golgi apparatus/body	2
1 (c)	Worked out as: magnification = $\frac{\text{image}}{\text{actual}}$ Magnification is $\frac{90\,000}{20} = \times 4500$	2
1 (d)	25 nm	1
1 (e)	$\frac{4}{3} \times (3.142 \times 64)$ $= 268.12\ \mu m^3$	2
1 (f)	Making ATP via aerobic respiration (either 'ATP' or 'aerobic' earns a mark because it is detail learnt at A-level. The fact that it is 'respiration' was already covered at GCSE).	1
1 (g)	This is a thin section / They have been cut/sliced/sectioned in a different plane	1
		Total 11
2 (a)	Interphase. (S phase is an even more accurate answer.)	1
2 (b)	DNA must double so that each daughter cell gets an equal amount after cell division.	2
2 (c)	In each new DNA molecule, one strand is original and one is new.	1
2 (d)	Mixture is spun in a super gravitational field so that the components separate out according to their density.	2
2 (e)	$^{14}N/^{15}N$ DNA is less dense than $^{15}N/^{15}N$.	1
2 (f)	One band at mid level and one higher up on the N^{14}/N^{14} line. Reason: two of the new strands will be all new/all N^{14}/N^{14} and two will be N^{14}/N^{15}	2, 1 for answer, 1 for reason
		Total 9
3 (a)	-COOH	1
3 (b)	2	1
3 (c) (i)	It only catalyses one particular reaction.	1
3 (c) (ii)	The proteins are different but they are still made up of the same 20 amino acids. It is possible for any of them to have an Arg next to a Lys, and so be cut by trypsin.	2
		Total 5
4 (a)	pH (the independent variable is the factor that is varied).	1
4 (b)	The rate of reaction (the time taken to digest the starch).	1
4 (c)	Any three from: Same temperature throughout; Same volume and concentration of buffer; Same volume and concentration of enzyme; Same volume and concentration of starch.	3, 1 for each

Question	Answer	Marks
4 (d)	Add some (yellow/brown) iodine solution. If it goes blue/black, there is still some starch there.	2
4 (e)	Repeat the experiment with boiled enzyme. This shows that it was the enzyme, and not the buffer or any other factor, that was digesting the starch.	2
4 (f)	Amount of product made per unit time (or amount of substrate used up per unit time)	1
4 (g)	0.95 – 0.75 in 100 seconds $= \frac{0.2}{100}$ $= 0.002\ M\ dm^{-3}\ s^{-1}$ There will be a range of acceptable answers.	2
4 (h)	Line starts at 1.0 and then reduces to almost 0, a mirror image of the product graph	1
		Total 13
5 (a)	Meiosis: Either: there are two cell divisions, or, the DNA content of the cell is halved.	2
5 (b)	The DNA has replicated/copied itself.	1
5 (c)	Cytokinesis/cytoplasmic division.	1
5 (d)	They will be double chromosomes (which means each chromosome consists of two chromatids), one from each homologous pair/a single set. (NB they will not be single chromosomes – that doesn't happen until the second meiotic division.)	2
		Total 6
6 (a)	Short interphase, or, interphase only as long as prophase.	1
6 (b)	Any two from: Chromatids are pulled apart; By the spindle fibres; One set of chromatids moves to each pole.	2, 1 for each point
6 (c)	It is quick/the shortest phase.	1
6 (d)	Any 2 from: No visible chromosomes; No spindle; DNA exists as chromatin; Nuclear membrane present.	2
6 (e)	46 (or 23 pairs)	1
6 (f)	Any three from: Genes that control cell division/oncogenes mutate; Tumour supressor genes mutate; Cell loses control of cell division; Mitosis out of control; Mass of cells/tissue develops.	3, 1 for each point
		Total 10

Question	Answer	Marks
7 (a)	Lipase	1
7 (b)	The carbon/hydrocarbon chain	1
7 (c)	The length of the carbon chain/number of carbons The degree of saturation/number of C=C double bonds	2
7 (d)	The free fatty acids lower the pH	1
7 (e)	All the substrate is used up	1
7 (f)	To calculate the rate at 4 minutes: The pH drops from 8 to 5.25 in 4 minutes, so the rate is $\frac{(8-5.25)}{4} = \frac{2.75}{4} = \underline{-0.69\ \text{pH min}^{-1}}$ (Remember that it's a negative value, because the pH is falling) The rate at 10 minutes is obtained by drawing a tangent You should get a value of around $\underline{-0.17\ \text{pH min}^{-1}}$ Ratio = 0.69/0.17 = 4.05 (ratios do not have units) The rate at 4 minutes is around 4 times faster than it is at 10 minutes. Any value around 4 will be acceptable.	3
		Total 9
8 (a)	A substance/protein that stimulates the production of a particular antibody; Or: A substance not normally found in the host body, that stimulates the immune response.	1
8 (b)	Any four from: Vaccine contains antigen/pathogen; Stimulates the primary immune response; Leads to the production of memory cells; If pathogen encountered, body produces antibodies quickly; Immunity lasts as long as the memory cells do.	4
8 (c)	Any two from: Virus constantly mutates/makes new strains; New proteins/antigens on surface/antigenic variation; Existing antibodies/memory cells ineffective.	2
8 (d)	Some parents perceive risk of potential side-effects, for example, allergic reaction, autism.	1
8 (e)	Any two from: When treatment is urgent/no time for body to make own antibodies; Antibody production takes time/weeks, for example, snake bites.	2
		Total 10

9

	Diffusion	Osmosis	Facilitated diffusion	Active transport
Takes place against a diffusion gradient	×	×	×	√
Requires metabolic energy from the cell	×	×	×	√
Requires a partially permeable membrane	×	√	√	√
Requires specific proteins in the membrane	×	×	√	√

		1 mark for each correct column
		Total 4

Glossary

α glucose (alpha glucose)	A form (isomer) of the simple sugar (monosaccharide) glucose. The polysaccharides starch and glycogen are polymers of α glucose.
α helix	A common type of secondary structure in a protein/polypeptide chain. The polypeptide chain forms a spiral for a specific length within the molecule
Accuracy	A measure of how close the data is to the actual true value. Note the difference between accuracy and precision. If a man is 1.81 m tall, a measurement of 1.743 m is precise but not accurate. The difference between accurate and precise is illustrated below:

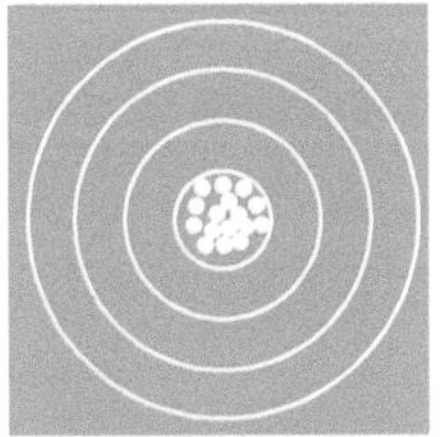
Precise-Accurate

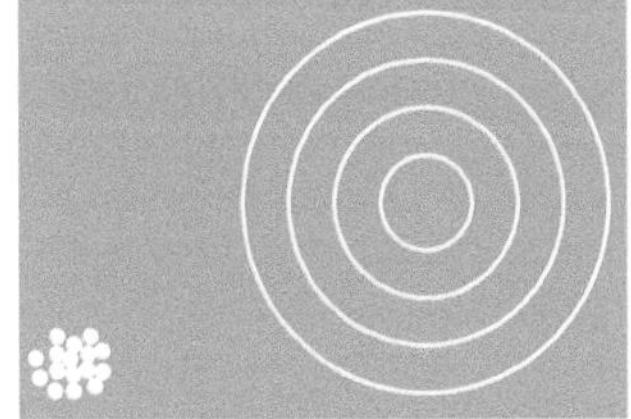
Precise-Inaccurate

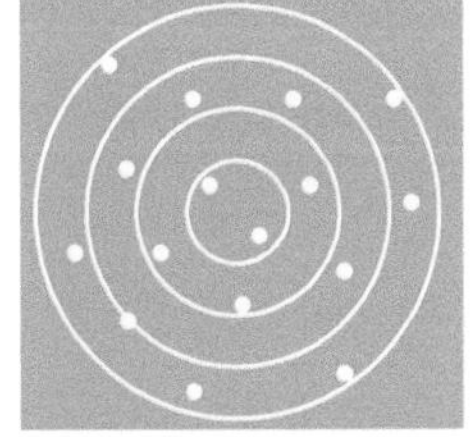
Imprecise-Accurate

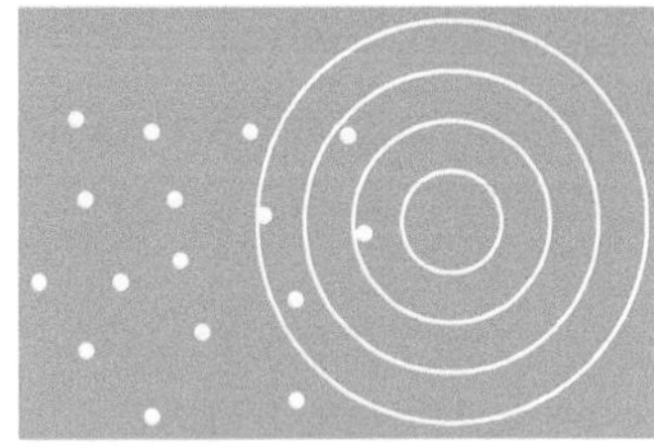
Imprecise-Inaccurate

Actin	Fibrous protein found in muscles. Combines with myosin to bring about muscle contraction.
Activation energy	Energy required to start a reaction: the energy needed to break bonds in the reactants before new ones can form to make the products.
Active immunity	Immune response in which an individual makes their own antibodies to combat a particular infection. Compare with *passive immunity*.
Active site	Catalytic centre of an enzyme: pocket/groove on the surface of an enzyme into which a substrate fits. The active site and substrate have complementary shapes.
Active transport	Movement of particles across a membrane against a diffusion gradient. Requires specific membrane proteins and energy (from ATP).
Amino acid	Building block of a protein. There are 20 different amino acids in living things. All have three-letter abbreviations, for example, valine, proline, serine (Val, Pro, Ser).
Amylopectin	Branched polymer of glucose: one of the two types of polysaccharide that make up starch. See also *amylose*.
Amylose	Unbranched polymer of glucose: one of the two types of polysaccharide that make up starch. See also *amylopectin*.
Anaphase	Phase of mitosis in which the chromatids split (at the centromere) and are pulled to opposite poles by the spindle fibres.
Antibody	In immunity, a specific protein made by a B lymphocyte in response to a particular antigen.
Antigen	Proteins and glycoproteins in a cell-surface membrane that are specific to a particular cell type.

Antigen-presenting cell	A cell that displays antigens in a form that T cells can recognise.
Antigenic variation	When the proteins on the outer layer/membrane of a pathogen such as the 'flu virus change in a short space of time/within a few generations. Caused by rapid mutation of the genetic material. The relevance is that antibodies made against one strain of the pathogen won't be effective once there are new antigens on the outer surface, so new vaccines need to be developed.
ATP	Adenosine triphosphate. Compound that acts as immediate energy source for metabolic reactions. *Respiration* makes ATP from ADP and phosphate; many other processes use ATP, such as muscular contraction, active transport.
Attachment proteins	Generally – any proteins in the cell surface membrane whose function is attachment to other molecules or to other cells. Specifically – proteins on the outer coat of a virus which allows them to bind to the surface proteins of particular host cells. If a virus cannot bind, it cannot gain entry to the cell.
β glucose (beta glucose)	A form (isomer) of the simple sugar (monosaccharide) glucose. Cellulose is a polymer of β glucose.
β pleated sheet	One of the two commonest types of secondary structure within a polypeptide or protein. See also α *helix.*
B lymphocytes (B cells)	Lymphocytes involved in the humoral response to an antigen; an activated B cell can produce both plasma cells and memory cells.
Base	In nucleic acids (DNA and RNA), one of four nitrogen-containing compounds, that fit together like jigsaw pieces. In DNA there are Adenine, Thymine, Guanine and Cytosine (C bonds to G, A to T). RNA has Uracil (U) instead of Thymine.
Binary fission	The process by which prokaryotic cells divide.
Buffer solution (or **Buffer)**	Solution that resists any change in pH. Acids or bases can be added to a buffer and the pH will stay constant (within the limits of the buffer).
Calibration curve	This is a method for determining the concentration of unknown solutions using a graph prepared from known values. The curve is often a straight line. For example, a colorimeter can be used to measure the absorbance (depth of colour) of solutions of known concentration. When given an unknown solution, you can measure its absorbance and then estimate its concentration by interpolation ('reading between the points').
Capsid	The protein coat that encloses virus particles.
Carrier proteins	One of the two major types of protein (the other being a channel protein) that transport solute particles across a cell membrane. Carrier proteins bind to the molecule to be transported and undergo a conformational (shape) change so that the molecule is moved to the other side of the membrane.
Catalyst	Substance that speeds up a particular reaction but remains unchanged at the end of the reaction. Enzymes are biological catalysts.
Cell fractionation	Method of separating out the components of a cell to get a pure sample of nuclei, or mitochondria, for example. Usually achieved by homogenising (mashing up) cells and then using a high speed centrifuge.

Cell recognition	An essential concept in the immune system. The cells of the immune system need to be able to recognise self and non-self, which they do by the proteins, or combination of proteins, on the cell's surface membrane.
Cell-surface membrane	A barrier that separates the contents of the cell from its surroundings, while still selectively allowing substances to move in and out of the cell. See also *fluid mosaic model.*
Cell wall	Outer protective coat secreted by cells of certain organisms. Plants always have cell walls made of cellulose.
Cellular response	An immune response involving T cells.
Cellulase	Enzyme that breaks down cellulose.
Cellulose	Unbranched polymer of β glucose. Forms long chains that bond to parallel chains via hydrogen bonds, forming fibres of great strength. Found in plant cell walls. Major component of paper, wood and cotton.
Centrifuge	Device that separates out the components of a mixture according to their density. The mixture is spun, creating a super-gravitational field. The densest component is forced to the bottom of the tube, forming the sediment.
Centromere	The point of attachment of two chromatids on a double chromosome.
Channel proteins	One of the two major types of protein (the other being a carrier protein) that transport solute particles across a cell membrane. Channel proteins basically form pores through which specific particles can pass. Unlike carrier proteins, they do not change their shape or bond to the molecule to be transported.
Chloroplast	Plant organelle that is the site of photosynthesis. Internal membrane system (grana) provides a large surface area to house chlorophyll.
Cholesterol	Lipid component of some cell membranes. Important in the development of atheroma.
Chromatid	One half of a double chromosome (present at the start of cell division).
Chromatin	'Spread out' DNA in the nucleus of a non-dividing cell.
Chromosome	Condensed mass of DNA that appears just before cell division. Each chromosome is one super-coiled DNA molecule containing thousands of genes.
Clonal selection	A process in which T cells divide by mitosis to form a clone of identical T cells.
Clone	An identical genetic copy. It is possible to clone DNA strands, cells or whole organisms.
Cohesion	The way in which molecules 'stick' together.
Collagen	Tough fibrous protein. Gives strength to tissues such as bone, cartilage, tendon.
Colorimeter	Device that measures intensity of colour or cloudiness (turbidity) in a solution. Gives a reading as percentage transmission or absorbance. A reference standard of pure water would give 100% transmission, or 0% absorbance.
Competitive inhibitors	Molecules that bind to the active site in an enzyme but no reaction takes place. Part of the inhibitor molecule will usually be similar in shape to the substrate.
Condensation	Reaction in which two molecules join, forming water in the process. Carbohydrates, lipids and proteins are all made by condensation reactions.

Co-transport	Transport across a cell membrane in which the movement of one substance relies on the movement of another in the same direction. For example, glucose is co-transported with sodium.
Cytokinesis	The process by which the cell splits in half after mitosis.
Cytoplasm	The fluid material in a cell, made up of proteins and other substances dissolved in water, and all the organelles in the cell (except the nucleus)
Cytotoxic T cells	Cells that destroy cells which have been infected by the pathogen that carried the specific antigen to which it can respond.
Diffusion	Molecular mixing, where particles in a gas or liquid move from an area of high concentration to an area of lower concentration until evenly spread
Dilution series	A method of producing a series of progressively less concentrated solutions (of higher water potential) by systematically adding water to a stock solution. This is can be done arithmetically (for example, changing the proportion of volumes of water and 1 M sucrose solution in a total volume of 10 cm^3) or more commonly, geometrically (e.g. by serially diluting by a factor of one in ten - you only need to do this six times to get a solution that is one millionth of the strength of the original).
Dipeptide	Molecule formed when two amino acids join by a peptide link.
Dipole	The separation of positive and negative charges.
Disaccharide	Molecule formed when two monosaccharides join by a glycosidic link. Common examples include maltose, lactose and sucrose.
Disulphide bridge	Strong S=S bond formed in proteins: occurs where two cysteine residues are close together. Important in maintaining tertiary structure, especially in fibrous proteins, e.g. keratin.
DNA polymerase	Key enzyme in DNA replication. Catalyses the addition of complementary nucleotides on the exposed strands.
DNA replication	The copying of DNA molecules. The two strands unwind and act as templates for the creation of two identical copies. Tales place in interphase, before cell division.
ELISA test (enzyme-linked immunosorbant assay)	A test used to detect a particular substance (such as an antigen) using monoclonal antibodies
Endocytosis	Uptake of material by a cell. Either solids (phagocytosis) or liquids (pinocytosis) are absorbed in a sphere of membrane. Opposite of exocytosis.
Endoplasmic reticulum	A network of membrane-bound channels found in the cells of eukaryotic organisms.
Enzymes	Catalysts (usually proteins) produced by cells, which control the rate of reaction in cells.
Enzyme-substrate complex	Combination of enzyme and substrate that exists for a very brief moment, after which there is an enzyme-product complex, and then separate enzyme and product.
Ester bond	Link between glycerol and a fatty acid found in triglycerides and phospholipids.
Eukaryotic	One of the two major cell types. Compare with prokaryotic. Eukaryotic cells are large and show more complex internal organisation and organelles.

Exocytosis	Movement of small volumes of material out of a cell. Vesicles fuse with the membrane releasing the vesicle contents outside the cell.
Facilitated diffusion	Diffusion speeded up by specific membrane proteins. Occurs down a diffusion gradient and therefore does not need energy from the cell.
Fatty acid	An organic acid with a –COOH group. Also called a carboxylic acid. Fatty acids vary in the number of carbons in their chain and the degree of saturation (the number of C=C bonds).
Fluid mosaic	Model of cell membrane structure: a continuous fluid double layer of phospholipids into which a random mosaic of proteins is studded.
Genetic code	The base sequence of the DNA molecule. The code is copied onto molecules of mRNA and used as a template to make polypeptides/proteins.
Glycogen	Main storage carbohydrate in animals. A highly branched polymer of α glucose, similar to amylopectin. Particularly abundant in liver and muscles.
Glycolipid	Composite molecules that are part lipid and part carbohydrate.
Glycoprotein	Composite molecules that are part protein and part carbohydrate.
Glycosidic bond	Bond between two monosaccharides, for example, glucose–glucose.
Golgi apparatus	A group of membrane-bound cavities that packages synthesised proteins into membrane-bound vesicles.
Growth phase	Part of interphase, which is, in turn, part of the cell cycle. In the G1 phase the cell increases in size as it makes new organelles and cytoplasm. If the cell is going to divide there is a second growth phase, G2, in which it makes enzymes and other proteins essential to cell division.
Haemoglobin	Protein found in the red blood cells of vertebrates, and in the body tissues of some invertebrates. Key function; storage and transport of oxygen; it binds to oxygen when abundant, and releases it when levels are low.
Helicase	Class of enzyme that unwinds and separates the two strands of DNA prior to replication or transcription.
Helper T cell	A T cell that helps other cells in the immune system by recognising foreign antigens.
Histones	In eukaryotic cells, histones are proteins that organise the DNA.
Humoral immunity	Also known as antibody-mediated immunity. When the immune response is due to the antibodies in the plasma rather than the cells themselves, as in cell-mediated immunity. (NB Humor = fluid, as in plasma.)
Humoral response	An immune response mediated by an antibody.
Hydrogen bond	Weak bond formed between hydrogen atoms and electronegative atoms, usually oxygen and nitrogen. Very common and very important: H bonds are responsible for many of the properties of water and are essential in maintaining the structure of proteins and DNA.
Hydrolysis	Literally 'splitting using water'. Reactions in which larger molecules are split into smaller molecules by the addition of water. Most digestion occurs by hydrolysis.
Hydrophilic	'Water loving.' For example, the polar heads of a phospholipid, which point outwards towards water in cell membranes.

Hydrophobic	'Water hating.' For example, the non-polar tails of phospholipids, which point inwards away from water in cell membranes.
Hypertonic	Having a lower water potential than another solution/cell.
Hypothesis	An idea that it is possible to test by experiment.
Hypotonic	Having a higher water potential than another solution/cell.
Immune system	Body system that includes the all the organs, tissues and processes that provide defence against disease. Includes bone marrow, lymph nodes, thymus gland, spleen and all the various types of white cell.
Immunisation	The process of generating resistance to an infectious disease by giving a vaccine. Vaccination and immunisation are the same process. See also *primary immune response* and *secondary immune response.*
Induced fit hypothesis	Model of enzyme action in which the enzyme changes its structure slightly when it combines with the substrate. Compare with the *lock and key hypothesis.*
Inflammation	Immune response to tissue damage. The area becomes red, swollen and painful.
Inhibitor	Molecule that slows down the rate of an enzyme-controlled reaction
Interphase	Part of the cell cycle – the period between mitotic divisions.
Isotonic	Having the same water potential as another solution/cell.
Keratin	Tough, fibrous protein found in skin, hair, nails, hooves and so on.
Latent heat of vaporisation	The energy that must be added to a liquid to change a quantity of that liquid into a gas.
Lock and key hypothesis	Model of enzyme action in which the substrate fits exactly into the active site on the surface of the enzyme. Compare with *induced fit hypothesis.*
Lysozyme	An enzyme produced by phagocytes that catalyses the destruction of bacterial cell walls.
Magnification	In microscopy, the amount an image has been enlarged. For example, x5000 means that the image is 5000 times larger than it is in reality. See also *resolution.*
Memory cell	In immunity, a long-lived white cell (B lymphocyte) that can divide when stimulated by an antigen to bring about a secondary immune response.
Metabolism	General term for the reactions that occur inside organisms.
Metabolite	The intermediates and products of metabolism.
Metaphase	Phase in mitosis where the chromosomes can be seen in the middle/equator of the spindle. Remember: meta = middle.
Microfibril	Literally, small fibre. Commonly applies to a bundle of cellulose or protein fibres. Examples of protein microfibrils include the tail of sperm, flagella, cilia and spindle fibres.
Micrometre (μm, or micron)	Unit of length. 10^{-6} m. 1 mm = 1000 micrometres.

Microvilli	Folds on the cell's surface membrane of certain cells, such as the gut epithelium. Microvilli greatly increase the surface area for cell transport, because there is more surface area and more proteins for processes such as active transport, and facilitated diffusion.
Mitochondria	The places in a cell where aerobic respiration takes place.
Mitosis	Type of cell division in which one cell divides to produce two identical daughter cells. Multicellular organisms grow and develop by mitosis.
Mitotic index	A ratio obtained by dividing the number of cells undergoing mitosis by the total number of cells in the population. When viewed with a microscope, the mitotic index is obtained by dividing the total number of cells in the field of vision by the number that are actively dividing (that is: ones with visible chromosomes). A high mitotic index may indicate cancerous tissue.
Monoclonal antibody	Antibody made on a large scale for medical use, for example, in pregnancy testing or cancer therapy. Produced by a hybridoma, a B cell fused with a tumour cell. Hybridomas are immortal, divide constantly and produce large amounts of antibody.
Monomer	Individual unit in a polymer.
Monosaccharide	Single sugar. Common examples include glucose, fructose and galactose.
Myosin	Protein found in muscle. Interacts with actin to bring about muscle contraction.
Nanometre (nm)	Unit of length. 10^{-9} m. One micrometre = 1000 nm.
Neutrophil	Most common type of white blood cell. General 'clearing up' cell whose main function is phagocytosis.
Non-competitive inhibitors	Molecules that inhibit enzyme reactions by altering the shape of the enzyme molecule. These inhibitors bind away from the active site, but alter the tertiary structure of the enzyme so that the active site is altered and enzyme substrate complexes cannot form.
Nucleic acid	Class of organic molecules that includes DNA and the various types of RNA. So called because they are weakly acidic and (originally thought to be) found in the nucleus. All contain nucleotides.
Nucleus	The largest organelle in a cell, containing most of a cell's DNA.
Nucleotide	Basic sub unit of a nucleic acid, consisting of a sugar (deoxyribose or ribose), a phosphate and one of four bases.
Organ	Collection of tissues that work together to achieve a specific physiological function. For example, kidney, heart, leaf, gill.
Organelle	Structure within a cell, for example, mitochondrion, chloroplast, ribosome.
Organic acids	Also called carboxylic acids. They always contain the functional group -COOH. Fatty acid is the name usually given to organic acids with carbon chains longer than about eight carbons.
Osmoregulation	The control of the water potential of body fluids.
Osmosis	The movement of water from a region of high water potential to a region of lower water potential through a partially permeable membrane.

Partially permeable membrane	A membrane that contains pores large enough for water molecules to pass through but not large enough for some solute molecules to pass through
Passive	Requiring no energy input from the cell (no ATP). Contrast with active (as in *active transport*).
Passive immunity	Situation where an individual has been given antibodies (for example, from its mother, or as a treatment for snake bite) rather than made it own. See also *active immunity*.
Pathogen	A disease-causing organism. Examples include bacteria, viruses, fungi, parasites.
Peptide bond	Bond that joins two amino acids in a dipeptide.
Permeability	The ability of a substance, such as a cell-surface membrane, to allow another substance to pass through it.
Phagocyte	A type of white blood cell that can engulf pathogens and subsequently destroy them using lysozymes.
Phagocytosis	Literally 'cell eating'. A process in which a white cell engulfs a bacterium/foreign particle and digests it, rendering it harmless.
Phospholipid	Lipid molecule consisting of one glycerol, one phosphate and two fatty acids. Key component of cell membranes.
Plasma cell	B lymphocyte that circulates in the blood making antibodies.
Plasma membrane	Alternative name for the cell surface membrane. Consists of a phospholipid bilayer and a variety of proteins (see 'fluid mosaic model').
Polar molecule	A molecule that has an uneven distribution of charge.
Polymer	Large molecule made from repeated units, called monomers. For example, starch is a polymer which contains glucose monomers.
Polynucleotide	A polymer of nucleotides, for example, DNA and RNA.
Polypeptide	Chain of amino acids. Proteins are made from one or more polypeptide chains.
Polysaccharide	Large carbohydrate molecule made from repeated monosaccharide units. Starch, glycogen and cellulose are all polymers of glucose.
Polyunsaturated fatty acid	Fatty acid containing two or more C=C (double carbon) bonds.
Primary immune response	Weak immune response following first exposure to an antigen/pathogen. Often not enough antibodies are produced to prevent disease symptoms. See also *secondary immune response*.
Primary structure	In a protein, the sequence of amino acids. For example, val-his-leu-his-met.
Primers	Short sections of RNA that attach to a gene before transcription or replication. They show polymerase enzymes where to begin reading the DNA template.
Prokaryotic	One of the two major cell types. See also *eukaryotic*. Prokaryotic cells are small and show much less internal organisation, no mitochondria, no ER.
Proofreading enzymes	Enzymes that check for base-pairing mistakes in DNA replication. They move along the new strand after DNA polymerase, removing any incorrect bases. This minimises the chances of mutations.

Prophase	First stage of mitosis, in which chromosomes condense, the spindle develops and the nuclear membrane disappears.
Protein	Large molecules made from one or more polypeptides (polymers of amino acids). Of fundamental importance in living things.
Protoctist	In classification, a kingdom of eukaryote organisms that contains the algae (including seaweeds), slime-moulds and a variety of single-celled organism such as amoeba and Plasmodium (the parasite that causes malaria). Sometimes called just 'protists,' this kingdom contains all the eukaryotic organisms that aren't clearly animals, plants or fungi.
Protoplast	A cell that has lost its cell wall, or has had it removed. Usually a plant cell, but can be bacteria or fungi. Usually done deliberately to allow manipulation/ transformation in genetic engineering.
Quatenary structure	In a protein with more than one polypeptide, the overall shape of the molecule.
Replicate	A repeat: for example, an experiment that is repeated is a replicate experiment.
Replication	Making a copy. See *DNA replication.*
Resolution	In microscopy, the ability to see detail. If a microscope has a resolution of 1μm, any objects closer together than one μm will appear to be one object. Generally, TEMs have a higher resolution than SEMs.
Reverse transcriptase	Enzyme that makes DNA from RNA: transcription in reverse, hence the name.
Ribosome	A small organelle; the site of protein synthesis.
Rough endoplasmic reticulum	An endoplasmic reticulum that has ribosomes on its outer surface.
Saturated fatty acid	Fatty acid with no C=C bonds, and therefore saturated with hydrogen.
Scanning electron microscope	A microscope that produces high resolution images of the surface of an object by bouncing a beam of electrons off the surface.
Secondary immune response	Rapid, effective immune response to a pathogen that the body has encountered before. Memory cells, long-lived B cells, divide very rapidly in the presence of such an antigen, producing large numbers of B cells that can produce antibody specific to the infection.
Secondary structure	In a protein, the particular shape formed when the amino acid chain folds and bends. Two common examples are the *α helix and β pleated sheet.*
Semi-conservative	The mechanism of DNA replication. In each new molecule, one strand is original (it has been conserved) and one strand is new. This was shown by Meselsohn and Stahl's experiment.
Sense strand	The side of the DNA molecule (in a gene) that is used as the template for making the RNA which is then used as a template to make a polypeptide or protein.
Smooth endoplasmic reticulum	An endoplasmic reticulum that has no ribosomes on its outer surface.
Solvent	The liquid in which a solute is dissolved to form a solution.
Specific heat capacity	The amount of energy needed to change the temperature of 1 kg of a substance by 1°C.
Starch	Main storage carbohydrate in plants. See *amylose* and *amylopectin.*

Substrate	Substance acted on by an enzyme, for example, the substrate for maltase is maltose.
Sucrose	A disaccharide composed of a glucose molecule and a fructose molecule
Sugar	Simple carbohydrate. Sugars are sweet, soluble white solids. For example, glucose, sucrose, maltose.
Surface tension	The way in which a liquid behaves as though there is a 'skin' where it meets the air, caused by the net downward attraction of intermolecular (cohesive) forces at the surface.
Synthesis phase (S phase)	In interphase, the time in which the DNA replicates before cell division.
System	Group of organs working together. For example, digestive system.
T lymphocytes (T cells)	Lymphocytes involved in the cellular response to an antigen; some T cells are cytotoxic, some T cells are helper cells
Telophase	In mitosis, the final stage of nuclear division, before cytokinesis. Cells in telophase have two separate nuclei, because the two sets of chromatids have reached the poles.
Tertiary structure	In a protein, the precise, overall, 3D shape of a polypeptide chain. Maintained by hydrogen bonds and sometimes disulphide bridges.
Thermophilic	Heat loving. Applies to bacteria that live in hot springs.
Thermostable	Resistant to break down by heat. Usually applied to a protein/enzyme that is not denatured by high temperature.
Tissue	A collection of similar specialised cells that work together. Four main tissues types in the human body are muscle, nerve, epithelia and connective tissue.
Transmission electron microscope (TEM)	The type of microscope where a beam of electrons passes through the specimen to form a high resolution image.
Triglyceride	Lipid consisting of one glycerol molecule combined with three fatty acids.
Tumour	A swelling caused when cells divide out of control.
Turgid	A pressurised plant cell. Most plant cells absorb water until the vacuole swells and pushes out against the cell wall, which resists any further expansion.
Turnover number	Measure of the speed of enzyme action. Defined as the number of substrate molecules turned into product by one molecule of enzyme per unit time (usually one second).
Ultracentrifugation	Centrifugation at very high speed.
Ultrastructure	Detailed structure of a cell.
Unsaturated fatty acid	Fatty acid with one C=C double bond. Can accept more hydrogen, so is unsaturated by hydrogen. See also *saturated* and *polyunsaturated fatty acids.*
Vaccination	Vaccination and immunisation are the same process. See *immunisation.*
Vaccine	Preparation made to stimulate a primary immune response. Contains antigens or pathogens, treated so that they don't cause the disease. Once vaccinated, exposure to the pathogen brings about the secondary immune response.

Vacuole	Fluid filled organelle in some cells. Particularly important in plant cells where it stores substances and provides turgor. See also *turgid.*
Vesicle	Small sphere of membrane inside a cell. Usually used to transport substances, for example, from the rough ER to the Golgi apparatus, or from the Golgi apparatus to the outside of the cell.
Virus	Disease-causing particle. Not usually classed as a living organism.
Water potential	A measure of the tendency of a solution/cell to absorb water by osmosis.
Xylem	Specialised conducting (= vascular) tissue in plants. Consists of dead hollow cells with strong walls made from lignin and cellulose. Function is to transport water and dissolved minerals from roots to leaves – the transpiration stream.

Index

Notes

Notes

Notes

Notes